5 Steps to Shooting

90% from the Free Throw Line

50% from the Field

40% from the 3-Point Line

Brian McCormick

180 Shooter / Brian McCormick

ISBN: 978-0-557-05861-7

1. Sports – Basketball. 2. Coaching. 3. Physical Education and Training – Basketball.
I. McCormick, Brian, 1976 –

Copyright 2009 © Brian McCormick
All rights reserved. No part of this book may be reproduced in any manner without the express written consent of the publisher. All inquiries should be addressed to:

Brian McCormick
info@180shooter.com

Published by Lulu
Printed and bound in the United States of America

Cover design: John Hayashi / Inkblot Creative Asylum / inkblot.ca@gmail.com

Thank you to my advisors on this project:

- Rick Allison: Founder/Trainer, Lone Star Basketball Academy
- Brianna Finch: Assistant Women's Basketball Coach, University of California San Diego
- Vincent Minjares. Individual Skills Trainer, Point/FWD Athletic Development
- Lindell Singleton: Author, *RAIN: A Workbook for Players who Want to Score*

Other books published by Brian McCormick:

Cross Over: The New Model of Youth Basketball Development
Blitz Basketball: A Strategic Method for Youth Player Development
Championship Basketball Plays
Developing Basketball Intelligence
Hard2Guard: Skill Development for Perimeter Players
Hard2Guard Player Development Newsletters, Volume 1
Hard2Guard Player Development Newsletters, Volume 2

Paperback books: www.lulu.com/brianmccormick.
E-books: www.180shooter.com.

Please visit 180 Shooter.com for resources, links, articles and information on individual workouts, shooting camps and clinics

Table of Contents

Foreword	5
Introduction	7
Part I: Shooting Basics	**11**
Chapter 1: **Shooting Psychology**	13
Chapter 2: **BELIEF**	21
Chapter 3: **General Movement Skills**	27
Chapter 4: **Shot Charting**	33
Chapter 5: **Teaching and Learning**	37
Part II: Shooting Progression	**42**
Chapter 6: **Phase I: Stationary Shooting**	43
Chapter 7: **Phase II: Movement**	53
Chapter 8: **Phase III: The Bounce**	59
Chapter 9: **Phase IV: Game Movement**	65
Chapter 10: **Phase V: Pro Shots**	73
Part III: Extra Shooting	**80**
Appendix I: **Common Shooting Flaws**	81
Appendix II: **Alignment and Shooting Biomechanics**	85
Q & A	87
Individual Drills	93
Team Drills	110
References	114

Foreword

I learned to shoot differently than today's players. I did not have a shooting coach; just a dad and a basket in my front yard. I did not play year-round on a team; I played in my front yard, at recess and at a local gym. I never had a shooting DVD, just ESPN and TNT.

I used many of the same concepts which I use when teaching players to shoot, but my motivation differed. I directed my learning. I created games against my favorite NBA players. I imagined their defense as I made moves and created shots. Today, I encourage players to use "imagery," "visualization" and "mental skills training," which are academic ways of telling a player to use his imagination. I never played against my favorite player because I thought it would help me improve; I did it because it was fun.

I remember the late 80's Michigan State vs. Wisconsin-Green Bay 1st Round NCAA Tournament game. Wisconsin-Green Bay was on the verge of the upset. Michigan State Head Coach Jud Heathcote called timeout to set up a play to get future NBA shooting guard Steve Smith a three-pointer. He dribbled from right to left toward the top of the key and made the game winning shot.

I remember the play because Smith dribbled left. I asked my dad why a coach would draw a play for a player to dribble with his weak hand. He explained that a lot of right-handed players preferred to dribble left into their shot because it is easier for them to square their body into a shooting position. As always, I took my ball into the front yard and tried it. Over the weekend, I shot several hundred game-winning shots dribbling from right to left with my left hand.

That was my learning process. I saw something, inquired and practiced. I saw things at practice, at camps or on television and went home to master it. I was never overburdened with instruction or evaluation. I shot in my front yard on my terms. If something worked, I continued. If it did not work, I either tried to fix it or I ignored it.

In this manner, learning was easy. It was a fun process which differed from the regimented school learning. Unfortunately, today's players grow up in an athletic environment where players are not allowed the freedom to learn on their own. The athletic environment is now as regimented as the school system, dominated by structure and adult-initiated activities. Rather than seeing a shot or move on television and trying it on their own in their front yard or at the park, players do drill after drill. The monotony kills players' curiosity and spontaneity and learning loses its fun.

Learning a skill, especially shooting, is hard and sometimes tedious, as I advocate shooting thousands of form shots. Drills are a part of the learning process. The players I train know they must hit a certain number of form shots in a row before we move to anything else. Sometimes the process is frustrating. However, mastering the fundamentals leads to new challenges, shots, moves and drills.

I shot close to the basket and mastered the basic fundamentals before imagining an NBA player's defense or imitating Smith's game-winning three-pointer. Nobody demanded that I shoot close to the basket or practice form shooting; I initiated my individual practice and decided what and how to practice. My driveway limited the distance, but not my imagination. I mastered the basic mechanics and used my curiosity and creativity to expand my skill. As I practiced, I thought about the performance. I concentrated on the feel of the move and the shot; if I felt something amiss, I walked through the move or shot and tweaked it slightly to create the proper feel. Without a coach constantly barking instructions and criticisms, I was more aware and in-tune with my practice and able to change and improve my own performance. I was self-motivated to practice because I enjoyed playing and practicing, whether in my front yard, at a team practice or in pick-up games down the street. Shooting was never work. My training was child-initiated, and the adult instruction I received occurred when I asked questions or sought advice from a more experienced player.

Introduction

In 2005, I published <u>Pure: The Biomechanics and Mental Approach to Successful Shooting</u>, which combined graduate school papers on biomechanics and sports psychology (visualization). <u>180 Shooter's</u> methodology differs, as it details the instructions and progressions I use as a professional shooting coach and incorporates research only to support the methodology.

I learn during every session. I study the way the body moves and the way players respond to instructions. I evaluate drills. I take notes. I have worked with very good shooters and beginners. Some start with dramatic flaws in basic movement patterns, let alone shooting technique, while others play professionally primarily due to their shooting ability.

I see basketball from both sides: professionals and novices. I have a unique appreciation and insightfulness, reflected, albeit at a different level, by the words of Anson Dorrance, the legendary University of North Carolina women's soccer coach, in his book <u>The Vision of a Champion</u>:

> "Back when I was coaching both the UNC and U.S. National Team, I would use the National Team to sort out what needed improvement for the American female player. I would bring those problems back to UNC practice field and try to solve them. Then, I would take the results and techniques for those UNC practices back to the National Team. In essence, we go to the highest level to see what the biggest problems are, and then we bring it back to the other levels, even to youth players from which the problems originate."

I use the mistakes made by college and professional players and discover solutions with the players I train daily. Through this problem-solving approach, I developed a methodology for developing a player over a series of years so he or she becomes a 180 Shooter: a player whose combined percentages from the free throw line, the field and the three-point line total 180.

Becoming a 180 Shooter takes more than a book or instruction. It requires effort. Shooting is a technical skill, much like hitting a golf ball. Tiger Woods did not become a champion by accident; he practiced purposefully and deliberately to become an expert golfer. However, shooting is also an athletic skill; one must be able to move and quickly decelerate with balance to go from horizontal speed to vertical power in a single plane without any declination or deviation. This requires balance, eccentric leg strength, core strength and more. Finally, being a 180 Shooter is a tactical skill, as shooting a high percentage requires getting open for good shots and knowing which shots to take and when to look for a better shot.

<u>180 Shooter</u> progresses through five phases from form shooting to "pro shots." The progression is gradual, and the best shooters master the shots in one phase before moving to the next. In any phase, I spend considerable time on drills and shots from previous phases; I constantly review the fundamentals before moving to tougher shots and more advanced instruction. A one-hour workout in the fifth phase may incorporate only 5-10 minutes of instruction, shots or drills from the fifth phase. That is how the game is played. A player shoots more free throws (Phase 1) than step-

back jump shots (Phase 5). Nobody completely masters shooting at game speed against defense under game pressure; therefore, incorporate the initial shots and instruction throughout the progression.

This book is not written for the impatient or those desiring a quick fix or magic pill. Becoming a great shooter takes work. The following is an organized progression to aid your journey towards successful shooting. However, without concentrated effort on the task, the book is just another that sits on your shelf. Any player can develop into a great shooter; you do not need massive strength or size or quickness. Shooting is basketball's great equalizer. While anyone can be a great defender if he or she plays with heart, passion and toughness, players with great lateral quickness and length have a definite advantage. Shooting is the one skill most accessible to any player, as it depends most importantly on a player's willingness to practice. Shooters aren't born; they're made.

How players should use this book

I wrote 180 Shooter to assist coaches with their shooting instruction, but individual players can use the book as well. I hope players use this book to self-direct their learning and improvement. One cannot rely solely on coaches or parents. Successful players take the initiative; they find ways to shoot more, whether before school or late at night. I hope every player realizes that shooting is a skill he can master if he has patience and a great work ethic. Becoming a great shooter costs little more than the price of a ball coupled with time, effort and sweat. On your list of priorities, how important is becoming a great shooter? Are you willing to do the work? Or, do you hope it happens magically?

180 Shooter features a "Shooting Matrix" for each phase. The matrix enables a player to self-grade his shot and determine when to move to the next phase. When a player reaches five on the matrix, he is ready to move to the next level as a maker, not just a shot taker, as he has developed the foundation to build upon when learning more difficult shots.

I developed the *180 Shooter Practice Tracker* (available at 180Shooter.com) to assist players with their shooting development. Training without a goal is just exercise. People who want to be great at a skill set a goal and track their effort and progress. The *Practice Tracker* is a tool to track one's shooting progress. Rather than keep notes in a notebook, *Practice Tracker* is an interactive program which makes the data accessible and usable for players who want to identify strengths and weaknesses from their practice sessions.

How coaches should use this book

Coaches always look for fresh material. I hope this offers new material, but also makes coaches think. Is it a new drill? Is it the progression of drills? Is it the instruction? I hope coaches use this as a reference and develop their own progression of drills, methodology and instruction. Success depends more on "how" you do things, not "what" you do.

On his blog, Stanford University professor Bob Sutton writes, "Creativity happens when people do new things with old things, either bringing old ideas to new places or creating new combinations of old things." This is the essence of coaching. There is nothing new in basketball. Creativity and innovation tweak or improve the old.

I hope coaches examine their teaching and consider their philosophy regarding shooting. I hope more coaches take a long term approach, rather than teaching step-back jump shots to 10-year-olds who struggle with lay-ups. I hope this book gives coaches the confidence that their ideas and thoughts are correct, despite what another coach or parent may say. Teaching shooting is not an event, but a long term progression.

180 Shooter features a "Shooting Matrix" for each phase. The matrix offers a way to grade a player's shooting technique and a method for moving players from phase to phase. When a player

reaches five on the matrix, he is ready to move to the next level as a maker, not just a shot taker, as he has developed the foundation to build upon when learning more difficult shots.

The *180 Shooter Program* helps coaches learn more about the shooting success and habits of their players. The *Shot Tracker Program* illustrates the shots that players take during games and their percentages from different spots on the floor. The *Practice Tracker* allows coaches to monitor their players' individual shooting practice to see if players practice the shots that they shoot in games. Through Shot Tracker, a coach can create a workout and send it to a player or a group of players to assist with their individual practice. When the players finish their workout and input their results into their individual Practice Tracker account, the coach can evaluate his players and their work and progress. Together, the programs enable a coach to structure his shooting practice and strategy to utilize players' strengths, develop players' weaknesses and put players in position to succeed.

How parents should use this book

Hopefully parents use the book to help their own son or daughter. Parents often tell me that their son or daughter will not listen to them. If true, support your child. Offer to rebound. Encourage him or her to go to the gym or the park and practice more. Use the drills to create a workout, or register at TrainforHoops.com to get progressive, individualized workouts. Do not try to be a coach; be a parent: a loving, supportive parent.

Players reject a parent's constructive criticism because kids want and need support and encouragement, not instruction or criticism. Most coaches and teachers point out flaws; players need their parents to balance this criticism. Several studies cited by the Positive Coaching Alliance suggest that a child's performance does not improve until he receives a ratio of five positive comments for every criticism. Unfortunately, most children hear more than 10 negative criticisms for every positive comment in the average home and classroom. Therefore, before they are ready for more instruction, they need someone to encourage them. Rather than playing coach and parent, separate the roles and be a parent. Rebound, track makes and misses, encourage your child and praise his or her effort and improvement, not just his success.

Second, I hope this gives parents a tool to evaluate potential coaches or trainers. There has been an incredible proliferation of shooting coaches and basketball trainers. Parents struggle to evaluate and differentiate the good from the bad. This book offers an example of a sensible progression; it is not the last word on shooting, but is an example to seek in a trainer or youth coach.

A trainer's worth is determined by his communication ability and the accuracy and timing of his feedback. However, these are hard to judge, especially from afar. When watching a trainer, one can see the workout's organization, the drill progressions and the methodology. Good trainers have sensible, organized, progressive workouts.

Instructions

180 Shooter outlines five phases of shooting instruction and practice. I purposely did not place age categories on each phase because the progression from novice to expert is personal and individual. Some players practice more than others. Some learn quicker. Some maintain task focus longer. Some start with bad habits which must be unlearned. Players differ and every player will use the following in his or her own way. 180 Shooter features a matrix at the end of each chapter which enables a player, parent or coach to grade a player's mechanics and establishes a benchmark for players to reach before moving to the next phase.

Players, parents and coaches tend to progress too quickly. We constantly compare ourselves and our kids to others and want to be at the front, not trailing behind. Rather than compare oneself to other players, contrast development over time. 180 Shooter is not a shooting book; it is a "making" book. Players may look advanced shooting threes and step-backs, but are they makers? Do they have the basic fundamentals to sustain development and promote improvement as they age? Or, will they hit an early plateau because their "advanced" skills are advanced for a young player, but not for a high school player, and the lack of foundation inhibits continued progression as they age?

If a 10-year-old makes three-pointers by shooting a two-handed shot from his chest, is he practicing a shot which will translate to success as a high school player? Or, is he sacrificing future shooting success for immediate results? A player who shoots a two-hand set shot from his chest eventually will have to change his shooting technique. It is easier to learn a new skill than to change an engrained habit. Therefore, sacrifice some shooting range early in one's development to develop shooting technique which translates as the player gets older and reaches more competitive levels. I grew up with a kid named Westy who was the best fourth grade shooter around. However, he never made a high school team because his two-hand set shot was too slow and too easy to block. In the fourth to sixth grades, he shot too well to change his technique. What coach would sacrifice several three-pointers per game to re-teach the proper technique for Westy's basketball future? He was great in elementary school, but his game never matured. The goal of this progression is to build shooting technique which transfers as a player grows and leads to success.

Very few players are 180 Shooters. During the 2007-08 NBA season, five players finished the season above 180: Phoenix's Steve Nash (190.3), Toronto's Jose Calderon (188.8) and Jason Kapono (183.2), New Orleans' Peja Stojakovic (180.8) and Utah's Kyle Korver (180.6). 180 Shooters are different. They do not fall into the comparison trap; they are not trying to keep up with the Joneses. 180 Shooters are disciplined and focused on their development, not others. They measure progress individually, not by comparing themselves to others. As John Wooden said:

> When you improve a little each day, eventually big things occur…Not tomorrow, not the next day, but eventually a big gain is made. Don't look for the big quick improvement. Seek the small improvement one day at a time. That's the only way it happens – and when it happens, it lasts.

180 Shooters progress gradually, mastering the skills and drills in one phase before moving to the next phase. They do not advance to tougher shots because another player did or because a "good" player should be in a certain phase at a certain stage of his development. 180 Shooters progress as makers, when they master the current stage. They move from Phase 1, which is form shooting, to Phase 2, which includes movement to the basket, when their form is perfect (5 on the matrix), not pretty good or better than some other players. Perfect.

In the late 1980's, Jon Spoelstra walked into a staff meeting with the Portland Trailblazers and asked, "What's it going to take to win a championship this year?" Most NBA teams do not think this way – they want improvement or to make the play-offs – but Pat Riley considers a season without a championship unsuccessful. Spoelstra writes, "Hooray for those who think, plot and dream to win it all *this* year." He challenges you to take an index card and write "What will it take to be the best____ this year?" and put the index card in your pocket and keep it there (Spoelstra).

How many players really think, plot and dream about being the best? How many write down their goals and look at them frequently? What will it take for you to be a 180 Shooter?

In some cases, the slow progression may seem boring or tedious. If so, maybe being a 180 Shooter is not an important goal. Maybe good is good enough. For a 180 Shooter, good is never good enough and the slow progression is a means to an end: 90% from the free throw line, 50% from the field and 40% from the three-point line. As one proverb suggests, "The juice is worth the squeeze."

Part I: Shooting Basics

1

Shooting Psychology

The five-phase progression outlines the physical path from beginner to 180 Shooter. However, the process requires psychological development. The way a player approaches learning and his ability to handle success and failure either enhances or handicaps his shooting development. Also, mental skills like visualization enhance the learning process and assist players in competitive settings.

The Three C's: Concentration, Confidence and Consistency

Great shooters develop the 3 C's: concentration, confidence and consistency. Concentration involves focus and control. It means allowing the body to work without interference from the mind. Confidence is trust and belief in one's ability. It comes from demonstrated ability. Consistency is conformity with previous practice. It means one's shooting technique is the same from repetition to repetition without variance.

The three C's are interdependent and intertwined. One cannot shoot with confidence if his shot is inconsistent; one cannot shoot consistently without concentration. Players need one to have the others.

Concentration

We have two dimensions to our attention: internal-external and broad-narrow. When our attention is internal, we attend to our own thoughts; when it is external, we attend to our environment through our five senses. When we have a broad attention, we see things through a wide angle lens; with a narrow attention, we zoom on specific details. With these two dimensions, we can characterize our attention in four ways: broad-external, broad-internal, narrow-external and narrow-internal. Everyone uses each style, but everyone has a dominant style. In pressure situations, we revert to our dominant style.

"Concentration involves fine centering your vision on the target…fine centering refers to a narrow focus of attention," (Mikes). Great shooters use a narrow-external attention style. They focus outward on the target. They do not allow their conscious mind to direct the shot nor does the crowd or opponent distract their concentration. Rather than thinking about their technique, great shooters rely on their subconscious mind. The mind directs the body's actions; those we do not think about (breathing, walking) are engrained in our muscle memory. Our central nervous system sends information to the muscles without conscious thinking.

When an experienced shooter struggles, oftentimes his attention is focused inappropriately. Rather than focus on his technique and trying to solve the problem, he should think less. "Here comes the Zen stuff. You're trying to control your throw and you can't. Don't aim…just look. Don't rehearse; just throw. Don't analyze; just feel. You have to center yourself and let the rhythm come. Once you do that…you can do all kinds of crazy things," (McDougall).

Early in the learning process, when a player's shooting is inconsistent, he must concentrate on his technique. In this instance, the player focuses his attention internally so he consciously alters his technique to shoot properly. However, once the player's technique is automated (Chapter 5), shooting is a natural act and the player must quiet his mind and allow his subconscious to shoot so that he shoots with more consistency.

Consistency

Consistency breeds confidence which breeds success. Peja Stojakovic, one of five 180 Shooters during the 2007-08 NBA season, admits that his shooting technique is not picture perfect; however, he attributes his success to the thousands of daily shots. His technique is consistent and his consistency breeds confidence and increases his concentration. When shooting with confidence, a player is less likely to worry about and question his technique.

When a shooter lacks consistent technique, it is hard to trust his technique. During the early stages, when technique is inconsistent, players should shoot close to the basket and make shots with proper form to develop confidence and consistency. As one's confidence and consistency increase, his shooting technique becomes more autonomous, and he can concentrate his attention on the target, not his body, increasing success. This success leads to more trust and confidence, and he can try new shots without worrying about failure.

Confidence

Shooters have bad days and suffer through slumps, but a great shooter's confidence never wavers. Shooters have short memories and always believe their next shot is good. "Life is a collection of self-fulfilling prophecies" (John Naber). Confidence is more vital to success than any technique. If a player trusts his technique, a shooting slump is temporary. However, if he lacks confidence – if he does not trust his technique – a slump can become a self-fulfilling prophecy.

In a 1982 study, psychologists Amos Tversky and Thomas Gilovich discovered that "there was absolutely no evidence of the hot hand. A player's chance of making a shot was not affected by whether or not his previous shots had gone in. Each field goal attempt was its own independent event," (Lehrer). However, some players allow a missed shot to affect their confidence, and they question their technique. When they question their technique, and shoot at a conscious level, they alter their technique, reducing consistency.

Developing the three C's, like developing one's shooting technique, is a process. However, if one fails to develop concentration, confidence and consistency along with the physical repetitions, one will never reach his peak as a shooter. Shooting is mental and physical, and the three C's are a part of a shooter's psychological development.

Developing the Growth Mindset in Young Players

Successful shooting requires confidence, but confidence requires demonstrated ability: it is the chicken and the egg. Rather than focus on makes and misses, develop the proper mindset in a young player. Stanford University psychologist Carol Dweck classifies two types of people: those with a Growth Mindset and those with a Fixed Mindset.

- **Fixed Mindset**: talents are fixed – you are born a good shooter
- **Growth Mindset**: talent develops over time and everyone can develop his or her skills.

People with a Growth Mindset tend toward a learning goal orientation, while those with a Fixed Mindset tend toward a performance or outcome goal orientation. Dweck characterizes the difference:

> "Students for whom performance is paramount want to look smart even if it means not learning a thing in the process. For them, each task is a challenge to their self-image, and each setback becomes a personal threat. So they pursue only activities at which they're sure to shine – and avoid the sorts of experiences necessary to grow and flourish in any endeavor. Students with learning goals, on the other hand, take necessary risks and don't worry about failure because each mistake becomes a chance to learn."

When I start with a new player, I ask him or her to concentrate on the shot's feel rather than the outcome. I direct my comments toward a learning goal orientation (effort/improvement) because growth and improvement are more important initially than the result. Unfortunately, outside expectations often pressure young players into an outcome orientation, as comments pertain solely to makes and misses (outcome), not improvement (growth/learning).

I trained two very different 10-year-old boys. Matt had a Fixed Mindset toward shooting; he would fall apart if he missed a couple shots. While most kids tend to shoot further and further from the basket, he would cheat and slide closer and closer. He was afraid to challenge his shooting range and risk missing shots. Aaron wanted to test his shooting with new and different shots. New moves excited him, while Matt seemed apprehensive or unsure. Aaron improved far more than Matt. He approached new challenges with a Growth Mindset, while Matt had a Fixed Mindset and feared mistakes or missed shots.

With a Fixed Mindset, the chances for improvement dim. However, with a Growth Mindset, a player believes he can make himself into a great shooter, increasing motivation and effort.

> "Research has revealed that in a motivational climate of mastery or task goal orientation, there are more adaptive motivational patterns, such as positive attitudes, increased effort and effective learning strategies. In contrast, a motivational climate of outcome orientation has been linked with less adaptive motivational patterns, such as low persistence, low effort and attribution of failures to (low) ability" (Gould).

Mihalyi Csikszentmihalyi concludes that "what characterizes people who use their skills to the utmost is that they enjoy the hardships and the challenges of their task. It is not that they are more likely to encounter pleasant experiences but that they persevere when they meet difficulties that would daunt others and occasionally succeed in turning experiences that others find meaningless or threatening into highly enjoyable ones."

In Dweck's research, one student faced a complicated puzzle, pushed up his sleeves and said, "I love challenges," which illustrates a Growth Mindset. These studies suggest expert performers (a term used by Florida State University psychologist K. Anders Ericsson to describe the experts in any field) develop the proper motivational strategies for success because they cope with failures and learn from mistakes without losing confidence. These strategies help the athlete maintain confidence when others lose it and persist when others quit.

Expert Performer Commonalities
- Greatest commonality is work ethic
- Parents expect them to do their best and work hard
- Values influenced by parents
- Attribute success to hard work
- Develop a learning orientation

Many athletes base their effort on others; they use the minimum effort to get the desired result. When teams run "line drills," the fastest players do not always run the fastest: they coast because they know they are faster than their peers and feel comfortable finishing in the middle. When challenged, these players answer, "I ran faster than so-and-so," or "I wasn't last." An expert performer does not coast; he sprints even if he wins by an entire court length. While an average player compares himself to his peers, an expert performer challenges himself to run his fastest. His work ethic and effort are not based on his peers, but on improving his own performance.

However, not every athlete with a good work ethic and high motivation succeeds. Some lose their motivation or work ethic, while others increase their drive, determination and effort. The difference is the way one explains his success or failure (Attribution Theory) and the factors which interact to determine his motivation (Achievement Goal Theory).

The Attribution Theory categorizes a person's explanation of success or failure into three categories:

- Stability: is the factor permanent or unstable
- Locus of Causality: is the factor internal or external
- Locus of Control: is the factor within his control

Motivation increases if the athlete believes the factors for success are stable, internal and in one's control (Gould). For instance, a player can explain a made shot in different ways:

- **Stable**: I made the shot because I am a good shooter.
- **Unstable**: I made the shot because I was lucky.
- **Internal**: I made the shot because I work hard every day shooting 500 shots after school.
- **External**: I made the shot because it was an easy shot.
- **In one's control**: I made the shot because I used proper shooting technique and shot inside my shooting range.
- **Out of one's control**: I made the shot because the defense played poorly.

If a player believes he made the shot because he was lucky, it was an easy shot or the opponent played bad defense, making the shot does not improve his future expectancy of success. Because he attributes his success to factors outside his control, success does little to improve his motivation or confidence.

Growth Mindset people have an internal locus of causality: they believe their effort determines their success, not their inherent gifts or traits. Maximizing their potential is within their own control and determined by their effort and opportunity.

Fixed Mindset people believe talent is stable. This increases motivation until one faces the inevitable hurdles. Then he questions his talent. A Fixed Mindset person believes success is out of his control and determined externally. When he is unsuccessful, he is not inspired to work harder, but is prone to quit because the failure means he lacks sufficient talent. Nobody reaches any level of success without hard work, so coaches and parents must encourage a Growth Mindset through comments targeted at effort and improvement, not the outcome or result.

Mental Skills Training

Mental skills training or mental practice helps players reach their peak performance. Mental practice primes the muscles for perfection and visualization exercises calm player's nerves and create a picture of success for the body to follow.

Mental imagery or visualization has several uses:

1. When learning a new skill, the athlete visualizes an expert performing the skill and attempts to replicate the performance.

2. To prepare for competition, the athlete visualizes certain possible events and prepares the mind and body for the actions to perform in the game.

3. During competition, the athlete calms the mind and visualizes success before a certain action, like a free throw attempt.

4. After competition, the athlete recreates plays that shaped the game's outcome to learn from mistakes.

Numerous studies confirm mental imagery's effectiveness. According to these studies, mental imagery primes the muscles for action or activates the muscles used. In effect, by imagining the event, one prepares physiologically for the actual event. The central nervous system does not differentiate between real and imagined events, so mental imagery acts as real practice, preparing the mind and body for competition just like physical practice.

Through mental imagery, an athlete creates an expectation of success. "During visualization, you are essentially priming the muscles for the action ahead…You condition your brain, nervous system, and body to perform in the way you want it to, thus increasing your chances of doing well in competition," (Baum). Through visualization, the athlete learns the proper movements for a perfect performance and conditions his muscles to respond accordingly. Through this imagery, an athlete responds more quickly to situations, providing a greater opportunity for success.

Jack Nicklaus said that it is important to visualize every shot before the attempt. A clear intention is important; one must clearly imagine the ball going in the basket and imprint the image in his mind. During a basketball game, the game's flow does not allow players to stop and visualize every shot. However, a free throw affords the time necessary to visualize the attempt and prepare mentally for the shot. Through a free throw routine that incorporates mental imagery and relaxation breathing, a shooter calms his nerves, prepares for the shot and dispels the pressure. He quiets his mind and allows his body to flow naturally.

Great players replay the game in their minds after the game. They recall plays just as if they were watching the game on tape. They use their senses to return to the moment and learn from the experience. Mistakes and losses become learning experiences because the players use the lessons, rather than ignoring the negative experience. They replay the situations and prepare for the next time they face a similar shot or play so they are ready to improve on their past performance.

Imagery requires practice, like any other skill. Start with a few minutes each day. Visualize a goal for the day. Create a clear, precise picture in one's mind before getting out of bed. Use all the senses: the more specific and detailed, the better. The more one practices, the better he will be at producing clear images in his mind. Once a player feels comfortable using imagery, he can use it before practice and competitions. Eventually, imagery can be most useful during games, whether before shooting a free throw or on the bench to prepare for action.

Sports are mental as well as physical. A player who hones only his physical side fails to train for peak performance. A better mental approach produces positive physical dividends. Most coaches believe their sport is at least half mental; however, when was the last time a coach spent half of his training time on mental skills? If these skills are important, why ignore them?

Players shoot and shoot and shoot, yet they shoot the same percentage every year. "Since the mid-1960s, college men's players have made about 69 percent of free throws...In 1965, the rate was 69 percent. As teams scramble for bids to the 2009 NCAA tournament, it was 68.8," (Branch). Of course, physical errors may prohibit dramatic improvement: every repetition reinforces a bad habit guaranteeing inconsistency. However, for players with good technique, stagnant shooting percentages stem from insufficient mental training. Concerted mental training increases their practice quality.

Mental Training Checklist

1. Know exactly what you want to accomplish before you start. In your visualization, allow yourself to feel as though you've already achieved your goal.
2. Keep your imagery personal, positive, detailed, and in the present.
3. Experience all the emotions and feelings that you possibly can. Keep all the images associated – that is, as if they are happening to you.
4. Don't force it. Your subconscious mind will guide your body to perform like the athlete you see in your mind. You should practice visualization, but let your brain and body do the work.
5. Don't expect instant results. Perform visualization once in the morning and once at night. Be patient and your skills will improve.
6. Don't expect visualization to compensate for lackadaisical approach to your physical training; you still need the physical practice of shooting the basketball.
7. Before a game or competition, run through your visualization exercises, reviewing what you want to accomplish (Baum).

Shooter's Mentality

Shooting's most important component is not the elbow or the legs, but the mind; Michael Redd's shot is not text book, but he is among the NBA's most prolific shooters. Redd's success is due to two things: supreme confidence and his ability to get open to take and make big shots.

180 Shooters never think about missing; once negative thoughts enter the mind, the chances for success lessen. Michael Jordan said: "I never looked at the consequences of missing a big shot. Why? Because when you think about the consequences, you always think of a negative result." Jordan was not a phenomenal shooter, but at game's end, nobody was better. The pressure never affected Jordan; it elevated his play, sharpened his focus. He believed he would make the shot, so a game-winning shot never added pressure. His confidence created a calm, which enabled him to make the big shots.

180 Shooters catch the ball in position to score. They move without the ball: the average player possesses the ball for an average of one minute per game. Great shooters are hard to guard without the ball.

180 Shooters think shot every time they catch a pass. They mentally and physically prepare to shoot. A shooter has to shoot, and great shooters possess this mentality. They catch the ball at the depth of their shot with body square to the basket intending to shoot.

180 Shooters anticipate and think a play ahead. While waiting to receive the pass and moving to an open spot, they gauge the proximity of the nearest defender and the speed of the closeout; they know upon reception whether to shoot; to take one dribble away from the closeout; or to pump fake and dribble to an opening. Great shooters have a feel, they anticipate, rather than react.

180 Shooters know how to read screens and the defense to create openings. Richard Hamilton plays like the Energizer Bunny. However, he doesn't just run around; he cuts with a purpose. He reads the defense and flares or curls; he sees and punishes the switch. He wears out defenders through constant motion and scores with his ability to find the opening.

180 Shooters beat their man down the floor to get easy shots in transition. They sprint the floor even when an immediate shot is unavailable to force the defense into a recovery, catch-up position, giving them the upper hand.

180 Shooters think like great shooters. They believe. Do you?

2

BELIEF: Shooting Technique

I use the BELIEF acronym to teach shooting. Belief reflects the importance of shooting's mental aspect and reinforces confidence and self-belief. Without confidence, a player will never shoot proficiently. "Shooting without confidence is like drawing water with a hole in the bucket," (Anonymous). The acronym explains the basic technique from the lower body through the hand placement and the mechanics.

- **B**alance
- **E**yes
- **L**ine
- **I**ndex Finger
- **E**xtend
- **F**inish

BALANCE: We know balance when we see it, but have a hard time explaining it. Vern Gambetta explains that "balance is essentially control of the center of gravity over the base of support."

Acquiring balance for stationary shooting is easy, as shooting is a bilateral skill with two feet on the ground. However, when we shoot on the move, attaining balance becomes more difficult, as it is the ability to reduce force at the correct time, at the correct joint in the correct plane in the correct direction for the required activity (Gambetta). Shooters stop their momentum to move vertically to shoot without declination (front-to-back movement) or deviation (side-to-side movement).

When starting with form shooting, start in an athletic position. A generic athletic position is one with chest and eyes up and shoulders over the knees and knees over the toes. If players are unfamiliar with an athletic position, use this exercise to create a general starting point:

- Bend and put hands on knees by pushing the hips back
- Pull shoulder blades together creating a flat back with chest up
- Move hands into the shooting position

Another alternative is to use a countermovement jump: a player starts with his hands over his head, swings down to generate power and jumps. After a couple of jumps, he stops at the bottom; this position is close to the base of his shot. A vertical jump is an expression of lower body power. A shot harnesses this power. When he bends to jump, his body naturally moves to the position from which it can derive the most power.

To check for a good athletic position, ensure that:

- Back is flat; no rounded shoulders or humpbacks
- Chest and eyes are up
- Hips are back
- Feet are flat, but weight is on the balls of the feet
- Knees are over the toes, not too far in front of the toes
- Weight is evenly displaced on each foot; no favoring one foot or the other, which is common when a player has an injury or failed to rehabilitate an injury like an ankle sprain and thus has reduced range of motion, even if there is no pain
- The player feels comfortable. This should be a natural position, not a forced position. Younger players may feel uncomfortable due to a lack of strength, especially core or posterior strength. Use core stability exercises like the plank to complement instruction.
- Use the cue words, "Drop your hips!" or "Sit into your stance!" rather than "Bend your knees!" when players need to acquire better balance or generate more power from the lower body. Rarely is the depth of knee bend the issue. Knee bend is inhibited by the lack of flexion in the hips. Teach players to bend by flexing the hips first with the knees following,

rather than bending the knees while maintaining hip extension, which creates an off-balanced position with knees in front of the feet.

EYES: Find a target and concentrate on it through the entire shot. Keep the head still and do not follow the ball's flight path. Some players focus on the front of the rim and some on the back, but I teach players to find a spot in the center of the rim. "You must learn to fine center on the center point of the basket…Contrary to what many coaches and experts say, your shooting target is not the rim itself, the front of the rim or the back of the rim. The true target is the center of the basket…the space within the circle of the rim," (Mikes).

Fine center on the middle of the basket: fine centering refers to the narrow focus of attention, while soft centering refers to a broad focus. A basketball player must alternate between soft and fine focusing: a point guard uses soft centering to see the floor. However, when he shoots, he fine centers on his target. The difficulty of shifting one's focus (visual acuity) is one explanation why great point guards are usually not exceptional shooters (with Steve Nash and Mark Price two notable exceptions), while great shooters are usually not noted for their passing acumen and vision (with Larry Bird a notable exception).

Be a two-eyed shooter (above). Do not allow the ball to obstruct your vision. See the target with both eyes.

LINE: Align the shooting toe, knee, elbow, hand and ball. The shooting toe points at the target with the knee over the big toe. The elbow is over the knee with the hand over elbow and ball over hand: one vertical line runs from inside the big toe to the ball. At the set point for a right-handed shooter, the right thumb points at the right eye. The elbow starts under the ball with the forearm in a vertical line. The hand and wrist rotate so the wrist points at the target at the set position (left). Everyone's anatomy differs, so these are general instructions. Great shooters are comfortable and the shooting alignment should not cause discomfort. Some players' shoulders are tighter than others, making a completely vertical forearm more difficult; some shoulders are wider than others, creating a wider stance. However, as a general instruction, aim for the alignment of the shooting toe, knee, elbow, hand and ball.

As the line illustrates, my set point is not a perfect vertical line. My stance is wider than shoulder width, which is one reason my shot line is inside my knee and big toe. My arm is close to a vertical line; I do not advocate forcing the arm past its comfort point just to get a perfectly vertical line.

INDEX FINGER: The index finger and middle finger split the center of the ball (next page left). At the finish, the index finger points to the target. In other sports, players concentrate on their grip (softball pitchers on the grip on the ball, golfers on the grip on the club), but in basketball, players ignore ball contact and hand placement. Splitting the ball's center with the index and middle fingers offers a consistent reference point; center these fingers because they remain on the ball the longest and provide the most force. With these fingers centered, spread the fingers, including the thumb. The thumb and the index finger form a "J," not an "L." Spreading the thumb creates a natural gap between the player's palm and the ball when the wrist is cocked into shooting position. This small gap keeps the ball firmly in the finger pads and calluses (right). Imagine there is a worm in the palm of your hand; don't squish the worm.

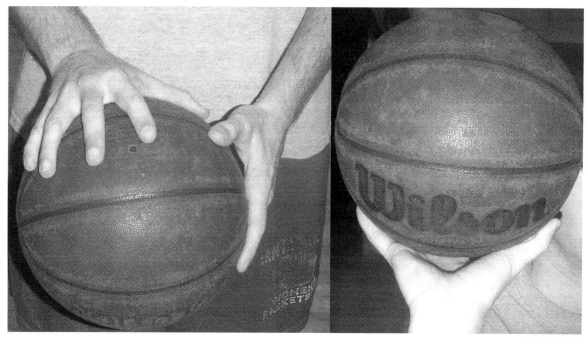

EXTEND: The entire body extends up and to the basket in a straight line. A good shooter never misses right or left: his shot is straight, a product of the elbow extending in a straight motion. Extension begins with the triple extension of the ankle, knee and hip joints and moves to the elbow. Start small (flexed) and end tall (extended). Some players shoot flat-footed; ensure the ankle plantar flexes. Some players do not extend at the hips, maintaining a slight forward lean in their upper body. Check for full hip extension to ensure the lower body power transfers to the ball. Full hip extension is erect posture.

FINISH: Shoot out of a telephone booth with elbow extending at a 55-60 degree angle. The off-hand stays on the ball until the shooting hand pushes toward the basket. As the elbow reaches near full extension, wrist flexion begins: the fingers push the ball up and to the basket. The off-hand falls naturally off the ball, imparting no force. After the release, the shooting hand falls forward naturally with index finger pointing at the rim. Fingers remain spread and relaxed through the entire shot. Follow through with the entire body, not just the arms; once the player enters the shooting motion, the body extends up and to the rim. On a jump shot, finish with feet slightly in front of the take-off point. On a free throw, end on the toes; if anything, step forward to regain balance. Finish the shot all the way; do not hurry for the rebound or to get back on defense. Hold the follow-through until the ball hits the net.

Extension and Finish

Shot Preparation and Shot Mechanics

There are two major shot components: (1) shot preparation and (2) shot technique. The preparation establishes a balanced shooting stance and moves the ball to the shot pocket. The shot preparation covers the Balance, Eyes, Alignment and Index finger. The technique unfolds from the shot pocket through the release, covering the Extension and Finish.

3

General Movement Skills

As I watch and analyze more players, I realize that almost all mistakes originate from a lack of balance. Show me a player with poor upper body mechanics, and I can point to a problem with his feet, balance or deceleration. At the 2008 NBA Summer League, I sat on the baseline. On the first day, the New York Knicks' Anthony Roberson was on fire. As soon as he caught the ball, the writers next to me thought that he was going to make every shot. Shooting on the basket at the far side of the court, I could only see his back — I could not see his technique or his hand placement or elbow or anything. However, by watching his body, I accurately predicted makes and misses. When his feet were set and he shot with balance, he made the shot. However, when he rushed the shot or did not square his body all the way to the basket or leaned to one side because he never fully decelerated, he inevitably missed. His misses had nothing to do with his shot technique in the traditional sense, and everything to do with his shot preparation and his inability to establish balance before shooting.

While most shooting instruction starts with the elbow or hand, most mistakes and weaknesses originate in the lower body. Insufficient lower body power production often produces an askew elbow; instability from too much knee bend without sufficient hip flexion results in a flat shot. If you attack the problem at the elbow or the shot's arc without reaching the problem's core, mistakes continue and frustration builds.

Players develop sports-specific skills quickly, but general movement skills lag. Many players have good upper body technique when stationary, but cannot shoot on the move because they cannot decelerate into a balanced position. Their technique falls apart. General motor skill development must precede sport-specific skills. The basic general movement skills in terms of shooting are: squatting and deceleration.

To squat properly:
- Initiate the movement by sitting the hips back
- Place weight on the balls of the feet, but keep the feet relatively flat (ankle dorsiflexed)
- Point feet straight ahead, not too far inward or outward
- Keep shoulders over the knees and knees over the toes
- Keep chest and eyes up

Several things may inhibit proper squat technique. To evaluate a player, use an overhead squat. The player holds a dowel with his arms outstretched over his head and squats, initiating the movement with his hips moving back and down. The two most common inhibitions are tight calf muscles and tight hips. However, for younger athletes, lack of posterior strength is a possible problem. As the athlete performs the overhead squat, identify the sticking point or the problem prohibiting execution of the squat:

1. The player's upper body leans too far forward. This usually means tight calves which impede ankle flexion. The torso moves forward to maintain the base of support. To remedy the problem, use a foam roll on the calves and stretch the calves before and after playing.
2. The player's knees cave in. This means the outer thighs are weak. Use a lateral tube walk to help combat the weakness.
3. The player's feet turn out. This means the outer calves are tight. Again, use the foam roll on the calves and stretch before and after playing.
4. Player loses balance and falls backward. This usually means a lack of strength in the posterior chain, either the glutes or hamstrings. Incorporate step-ups, lunges and back bridges to develop posterior strength.
5. The player bends onto his toes rather than sitting his hips back with his heels on the ground. This usually means the ankles or calves are tight. Use ankle rehab exercises like standing on one foot and drawing the alphabet with the other foot; use a foam roller on the calves and stretch the calves.

Practice the squatting movement before initiating shooting instruction, rather than teaching the squat as part of the shooting technique. During your dynamic warm-up, teach and train proper deceleration. Deceleration training helps prevent injuries and improves performance.

When running in a straight line, decelerate in one of two ways: (1) Lunge Stop or (2) Hockey Stop. The lunge stop is used to go from a sprint to a back pedal (or from a back pedal to a sprint), while the hockey stop is used when turning to run in another direction. The final step of deceleration is the first step of acceleration (Lee Taft). Otherwise, one can slow down indefinitely, like a sprinter after completing a race. In shooting, the shooter changes from linear deceleration to vertical acceleration.

Lunge Stop

- Used when running forward to stop quickly in the split stance or lunge position
- Lower the hips and stop the lead leg knee over the foot, like a lunge
- Shoulders should be more forward than a strength training lunge
- Back leg bends close to 90-degrees
- In live situations players do not hold the lunge position, but reactively push off to back pedal.
- The reverse lunge is done off the back pedal position with the rear or stopping leg much further back and the shoulders forward to accelerate quickly (Taft)

Hockey Stop

- Turn the hips, legs and feet so they are parallel with the end line, like when running line drills
- Outside leg is the final decelerator and is the most important leg to control momentum and to change direction
- Inside leg begins deceleration because in a normal stride pattern (r,l,r,l,r) it touches down first as the body turns (Taft)

As you look at the picture, I was running from left to right. I stopped right-left, with the left leg as the final decelerator. leaned into the stop and am ready to accelerate to the left of the base.

In Phase I, players train general movement skills without the ball. In Phase II, continue this training with the ball. Train deceleration as a separate technique, not just with shooting. If a player cannot acquire balance, the five-phase progression is of little importance.

I worked with a good free throw shooter who struggled to shoot with movement. Immediately, the discrepancy led me to study her movement and particularly her deceleration. She leaned back, slowing down over several steps rather than using a quick 1-2-step. Rather than drop her hips, she extended her hips as she slowed, creating a pushing motion on her shot. She never reached a vertical plane; she leaned backward as she released the ball, which led to an angle of release between 23-degrees and 37-degrees, far from her 45-degree angle of release on free throws and far below the optimal angle.

Once we discovered the problem, we exchanged the basketball for a medicine ball and she did a squat-and-throw. With the medicine ball under her chin, she did a half-squat, exploded upwards, and threw the ball. Next, because she struggled to transfer horizontal motion to vertical motion, she did three broad jumps before the squat-and-throw. Finally, she replaced the broad jumps with two bounds and stopped with a quick 1-2-step, not a jump stop. Starting on her left foot, she bounded to her right foot and then from her right foot to a left-right stop and threw the ball. She focused on dropping her hips and getting into an athletic stance to decelerate properly and apply more force on the throw. Next, we repeated these exercises with a basketball shot. First, we did a squat and shot; then we did three broad jumps into a squat and shot; and finally, we did two bounds into a 1-2-step and shot.

By disassociating the movement from the shot, she learned the movement rather than continuing to shoot with the same mistake. As she learned to drop her hips, and the movement became more natural, the transfer to her shooting increased.

I use many general movement concepts, but add the ball and finish in shooting position. We receive the pass on one leg, bound into shots, use broad jumps and more. To improve one's balance and eccentric strength, which enhances deceleration, implement single-leg training. These exercises are of a higher intensity and require a base level of strength, but a "bound and hold" trains body control, especially relating to deceleration. A bound is a hop from one leg to the other.

Bound and Hold

- Start on your right foot and land on your left foot (and vice versa)
- Absorb the force by landing on the ball of the foot and sitting into the landing
- Bend the knee and hip, but keep eyes and chest up
- Hold the position for a count of three before alternating legs
- Add a sequence with eyes closed to enhance proprioceptive awareness

Conditioning

When developing technique, quality of movement supersedes the quantity of movement or intensity. "Fitness is something that happens while you practice good technique," (Laughlin). Some conditioning is appropriate, but use short sets to prevent fatigue during the learning process. In the formative stages, fatigue interferes with proper skill acquisition. Practice good shooting habits rather than concentrating on the workout's intensity. If players are not practicing good habits, they develop bad habits, and fatigue causes players to train with poor habits. Develop the skill first and condition separately. After mastering the skill, combine shooting and conditioning.

A break down in form signals fatigue. While players must learn to shoot when tired, I do not want to create bad habits. I do sets of 6, 8 or 10 makes. If a player hits seven for eight and misses four in a row, I know fatigue hits around the eighth repetition. I add repetitions when the player finishes a set with only one or two misses; otherwise, he remains at the same number for the next set and in the next workout. My goal is not to wear out a player, but to help him learn to maintain his mental concentration and technique when fatigued.

The drill's intensity depends on the active rest. During conditioning-type drills, the intensity is sub-maximal; players do not run full speed. Between repetitions, they jog (sometimes a back pedal or shuffle). When the intensity increases, each repetition is a full sprint, game-speed shot. The difference is sub-maximal conditioning (like running a lap on the track) versus interval training (like running 40m sprints with near full recovery). Use each method to improve basketball conditioning.

Do not get caught in the "if some is good, more is better" thought process. Asking players to sprint-sprint-sprint so they are tired takes their concentration away from shooting. Focus on the objective; if conditioning is the primary objective, such as in the pre-season, work without a ball or use other drills. Use shooting drills to maintain conditioning in-season, to create game-like shooting situations and to build good habits when tired.

4

Shot Charting

Here is a familiar scene: a player walks onto the court and jacks a shot from three-point range; he chases the rebound and shoots again. This is his or her warm-up. I directed a clinic for 9-12-year-olds. I arrived early and watched every player warm-up. While I shot from no further than 15-feet and made several hundred shots, the boys threw up half-court shots, 360-degree lay-ups, and running three-pointers. The smallest player, the only girl, shot from no further than 10-feet and made a good percentage. When the clinic started, I said that she was the player I would choose for my team, as I knew she would improve. During the clinic, she understood the drills and moves despite starting near the bottom in skill level. She had good practice habits and listened well. She practiced shots that she could make and ignored everything else, allowing her to shoot with correct technique. Most young players do not practice in this manner, and they develop bad habits which must be changed later.

Learning a new skill is exciting; however, mastering it can be tedious. Most people lack the patience to start close to the basket every time. Early in the learning process, a player practices a good habit or develops a bad habit. Players who rush to the three-point line do so at the expense of proper technique.

When I coached at U.C. Santa Cruz, I worked with freshman Matt Glynn. Glynn broke his left wrist and committed himself to re-learning his shooting technique. It was a slow process, which was incomplete when he returned to action. At practice, he would not shoot three-pointers because he lacked the coordination with his new technique from that distance. On his free throws, his left hand never touched the ball: he practiced so many shots with a broken left wrist that he felt more confident shooting one-handed than with two hands.

Another player, "Hollywood," teased Glynn because he could not make a three-pointer. But, Glynn had a plan and worked every day to develop his technique. By season's end, Glynn relegated Hollywood to the bench, starting at point guard in the last game and shooting 16/17 from the free throw line and finishing with 32 points and 9 assists. During his senior year, he shot 50% from the three-point line and made 46 straight free throws. He was a 180 Shooter during his last two seasons playing for a top 10 NCAA DIII program and earned All-American honors.

There was no magic formula, except time, patience and work ethic. Glynn made himself into a shooter through his desire and relentless pursuit of perfection. The process required thousands of shots. He brought a notebook to every workout, and after each set, he wrote down his makes and misses. He tracked every shot in every workout.

He tracked his practice workouts so he could evaluate his progress. Without keeping track, how does one know if he is making progress? Without a firm goal and a way to measure the goal, a shooting workout is just exercise.

In my first years as an assistant coach at the high school and college level, we used shot charts to chart our team's shots during each game. The shot charts illustrated our shot selection so we could make adjustments at half time, if necessary, and after the game, we tabulated the results to measure our team and individual shooting percentages. One coach kept the charts by quarter so we knew our shooting results during different periods. I always assumed that every coach used shot charts to assist his players with their shooting development.

However, even at the NBA level – where assistant coaches are plentiful – shot charting apparently is not standard, at least based on the reaction of Washington Wizards' forward Caron Butler:

"Wizards forward Caron Butler attributed his career-high 21.5 points and .481 shooting percentage to the work of shooting coach Dave Hopla…One of the elements of Hopla's expertise is shot charting, *which is new to Butler and his teammates*. It allows a player to see the spots on the floor from which he's shooting well — or poorly. 'It lets me know what I need to work on,' Butler said. 'And with the percentage now, I know from the floor, I'm shooting like 80 [percent] from 16 on in. It gives me confidence. I can come to a spot on the floor and know it's a good shot. I can be like 'Coach, I'm shooting 80! It was a good shot!'"

Without tracking our shots, subjectivity affects our judgment. We remember emotional experiences because "emotional experiences register more strongly in memory than ordinary experiences. They get a special 'tag' because of the emotional charge associated with them. We're hardwired that way, a survival mechanism inherited from prehistoric times," (Parent). When a 10-year-old makes a three-point shot, we exaggerate his shooting ability. The make creates an emotional tag because it is a special shot, so we remember the made three-pointer. Meanwhile, when the same player misses a dozen three-pointers, nothing registers because we expect him to miss those shots. We inflate his shooting ability because we remember the one make and ignore the misses. Rather than encouraging him to shoot more three-pointers because we mistakenly believe he is a good shooter, we should encourage him to shoot shots that are more in his range. Otherwise, bad habits form as he attempts to replicate his three-point success.

Shooting coaches, like Hopla, chart shots so players understand their strengths and weaknesses. Knowing their strengths gives them confidence from that area of the floor or that type of shot, while knowing their weaknesses fuels the players' off-season training. The shot charts eliminate subjectivity. If a player shoots 80% from the elbow, then he knows to get to the elbow. However, if he shoots 20% on shots off the dribble, he passes on shots off the dribble until he has a chance to practice these shots deliberately in the off-season.

What is the difference between an average shooter and a 180 Shooter? Great shooters are obsessive about the numbers, the objective data. Glynn kept a notebook with every workout that he did in his four years of college. Hopla "has the notebooks to prove it. About 50 of them, going back decades…Why? Because he figures that if one's attitude is, 'Who's counting?' then, well, what's the point of doing anything, really? 'I'm addicted, to shooting and to the numbers. They go hand in hand,' Hopla says… 'I want to see myself getting better…To know for sure, you've got to write it down.'"

In the 21st Century, notebooks are outdated. I created the 180 Shooter Practice Tracker and Shot Tracker to replace the notebooks and make the information easier to sort, digest, evaluate and use. Individuals use the drills outlined in the back, write down their results during their practice and input the results into their program. Immediately, they are able to sort by types of shot, locations and more. They can see on a graph their improvement and also the consistency of effort.

The Shot Tracker program has dual uses for coaches. First, coaches can keep a shot chart (below) during games, input the results into the program and combine, sort and evaluate data over a period of time, by player or by type of shot. Also, the program allows coaches to design a workout and email it to their players. Once the players complete the work and enter their data, the coach can view the results and sort, evaluate and use the information.

Coaches can use the program to design more effective shooting practice to attack individual's weaknesses or use it to design a more effective offensive system based on the players' demonstrated strengths in games and practice. The *Shot Tracker* and *Practice Tracker* programs reinforce the learning progressions from this book and provide another source of information for players seeking to become 180 Shooters. Using a shot chart or a tool like the Shot Tracker program can help a coach make informed decisions about a shooter's ability, and also shape the shooter's practice in the off-season to attack any deficiencies based on the objective data.

Few teams have systems to measure improvement objectively. How do you know if you are improving if you do not track your shots? To maximize one's potential as a shooter, he must be obsessive about the numbers. This differentiates the average shooters who practice a lot from the great shooters who are committed to being the best. It is not a matter of what they do, but how they do it. The best shooters have a specific goal and they measure their practice to monitor their progress toward their goal.

180 Shooter Shot Chart

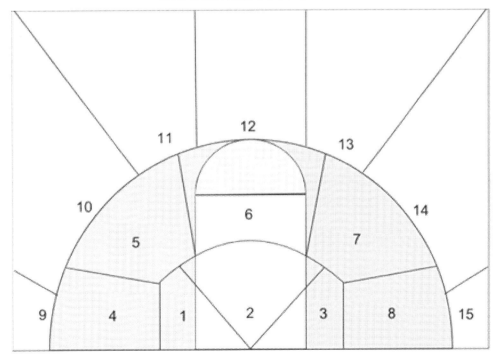

5

Teaching and Learning

When learning a skill, players progress through three stages of learning or skill acquisition: Cognitive, Associative and Autonomous.

The First Stage, or the Cognitive Stage, requires great effort and thinking by the player and is plagued by mistakes. The player knows he made a mistake mostly because he missed the shot, but he does not feel the mistake; he lacks body awareness. Skill performance is inconsistent and players rely on outside feedback. This stage is like the building of a computer, putting the parts together and preparing the computer for operation.

The Second Stage, or the Motor Stage, is characterized by greater consistency, but the athlete still thinks his way through the shot. The proper technique is not automatic, so he must concentrate fully on the exercise. However, during this stage, the athlete begins to feel and be aware of his own mistakes and can start to self-correct. This stage is like the programming of the computer, where all the code is written and the computer prepared to generate immediate responses.

The Third Stage, or the Autonomous Stage, is characterized by consistency of execution as the player shoots without concentrating on technique. His concentration centers visually on the target, increasing accuracy. He is fully aware and understands his mistake on the release, not after watching the result, so he can self-correct. Upon release, he knows whether the shot is good or whether it will miss short. He feels the shot and is completely aware; everything is automatic. This stage is the finished computer, when answers immediately appear or programs run effectively and immediately without complications.

While learning, drilling and mastering the proper technique, use the general and basic shots in Phases 1-3. Advance to the game-specific and more difficult shots once the basics are automatic. Transitioning to a new phase introduces new variables which create a new learning curve. The five-phase progression is not linear or constant. When a player transitions from stationary shooting to shooting on the move, he adjusts to the new variables. The feel differs for a stationary shot versus a shot on the move. In a sense, each time a player transitions to a new phase, he re-starts the learning process. However, at each subsequent phase, the time required to master the skill shortens because only the shot preparation changes.

Develop consistent, proper technique early to provide a foundation for growth and improvement. Learning perfect technique is just as easy as learning poor technique, but it is much more difficult to re-learn and change one's technique. Many college coaches will not alter a player's shooting technique, regardless of deficiency, because a college player's shooting technique is automated – that is, he does not consciously control his technique. Using the computer analogy, college coaches typically do their best with a broken computer. Maybe they buy a new computer (recruits a new player) to use on important projects (end of game situations), but use the broken computer (poor shooter) for other roles (defense, setting picks) like email.

Should a coach ignore a computer with a bug or virus and continue using the computer despite the glitch? What if the virus affects the computer's efficiency or accuracy? Wouldn't most people fix the problem, even if it requires reprogramming?

To improve, a player must concentrate on his technique to make changes. Change requires effort. Coaches leave players alone because they fear the initial step backward associated with shooting at a conscious level, or they believe the player lacks the work ethic to improve his shooting dramatically. "The only way you'll form long-lasting habits is by applying the Power of Less: focus on one habit at a time, one month at a time, so that you'll be able to focus all your energy on creating that one habit," (Babauta). How many players will work for 30 days straight and focus all their energy on only one habit?

In the summer of 2005, I worked with a college player who wanted to improve her shot so she could get her shot off at the college level. She was a set-shooter in high school, and shot a good percentage from the three-point line, but the shot was slow, and she could not shoot off the move or off the dribble.

During the summer, she played on an adult league team; previously, she had been the designated set-shooter. When her summer league started, she had not developed the three-point shot, and I did not want to interrupt her learning every time she played. I asked her not to shoot three-pointers. She listened. We started from the bottom, re-working her shot close to the basket and gradually moving further from the basket. The goal was to be as equally proficient from the three-point line at the end of the summer, but to shoot with a quicker shot and off the dribble.

I was in and out of town all summer, so she mostly trained on her own. She worked out every day and refrained from shooting three-pointers in her games. She was 100% committed to her shooting development. By the end of summer, she shot the same percentage as before, but she shot much quicker.

Babauta's challenge is similar to Florida State University Professor K. Anders Ericsson's deliberate practice. According to Ericsson, players need approximately 40 hours to play a game at an acceptable level. After this period, playing has minimal effect on skill development. At this point, players need what Ericsson terms "deliberate practice." Deliberate practice requires a specific goal, concentration and immediate feedback (Ericsson). During games, players perform skills at an unconscious level; however, improvement requires altering the performance at a conscious level. Improvement occurs when players attack a specific skill with concentration and immediate feedback.

> **Babauta's Challenge**
> 1. Select one habit.
> 2. Write down your plan. Specifically state your goal each day.
> 3. Report on your progress daily.

When players' minds wander, they lack the attention necessary to concentrate on the specific objective; without the concentration, players work on auto-pilot, maintaining the same flaws. The coach must provide feedback so players feel the difference between a correct repetition and an incorrect repetition; players must learn the difference so they can self-correct and provide their own feedback based on the shot's feel.

Practice makes permanent. Shooting drills done without a specific task, immediate feedback or player concentration ingrain the current shooting habits. Getting better at shooting poorly is not the goal, but it is often the manner in which we practice. To alter or change performance and habits, players must train at a conscious level to override the automatic skills. They need to re-train new habits and correct shooting technique, which takes effort and concentration.

Body Awareness

An overlooked aspect of coaching is preparing players to perform without the coach. A coach's feedback is useful and important, especially during the Cognitive Stage. Players who rely solely on the coach to correct mistakes never take responsibility for their own learning, development and improvement and never fully maximize their talent. To enhance a player's learning teach him to self-correct his mistakes through developing body awareness. "The teaching mission of the guru is an attempt to free his followers from him," (If You Meet the Buddha on the Road, Kill Him!).

Rather than give players the answers, question players:

- Did you feel your hand on the follow-through?
- Do you know why you missed the shot?
- Where have the last three shots missed?
- Where was your foot when you stopped?

Start with low order questions (yes/no) and progress to higher order questions which require the player to think, understand and explain. Once players develop some body awareness and familiarity with the questioning approach use higher order questions which make the player think or analyze his performance to answer, rather than nodding or answering yes or no.

If a player does not know the answer, guide the player by telling him or her where to concentrate on the next shot:

- Pay attention to your follow-through and tell me what you feel
- See where your lead foot is when you catch the ball

Students retain more information when they discover the answers. Use questions to help players retain information and gain body awareness rather than relying on the coach. Some players want a coach to do everything. These players must understand the necessity of body awareness, as a player unaware of his body position prior to the shot or his hand movement during the shot cannot expect to be a good shooter. Without body awareness, or this feel, how can a player constructively use a missed shot to prevent the same mistake? Without body awareness, how can a player develop a consistent shooting technique?

Another technique is to have the player verbally locate the shot after the release. Many players do this, yelling, "Short!" as they release the shot. Use this technique to gauge the player's body awareness. If his assessment is accurate, he has good awareness. If he has no idea, his body awareness is poor and his technique is likely inconsistent, which means he is in the Cognitive Stage. Players who correctly predict the outcome, but cannot explain the mistake, are in the Associative Stage, while those who predict and explain the mistake are likely in the Autonomous Stage. When players predict correctly, but are unsure of the explanation, use questions to guide the player to the answer. This takes more time, and is more difficult with a large group, but it is more effective.

As players develop a greater feel, talk less and reserve instruction for frequent mistakes or to check a player's perceptions. I watched an NBA player work out over the summer and he missed short on seven straight shots. After each one, he held up his hand and made a gesture as if something was wrong with his follow-through. However, his follow-through was never the issue; his problem was in the transfer of power from his lower body to his upper body. He never fully extended his hips, so he never got lift into his shots; he pushed the ball, rather than extending with the shoulder rotation and elbow extension.

This situation requires a coach's feedback to correct the player and focus his attention on the right area. After explaining the technique flaw, use cue words and questions, focusing the player on his hip extension, not his follow-through:

- "Do you feel the difference in the hips? What is the difference?"
- "What was your body position on your release that time?"

Asking players to replicate their body position is another tool for teaching body awareness, as well as improving a coach's effectiveness. Many times, coaches ask players to get in a lower stance. Players believe they get lower, but their expectations differ from the coach's. A coach can be clearer about his expectations, explaining, for instance, that low is a full squat, with the top of the thigh parallel to the ground. The specificity gives the player a reference point, as opposed to the vague instruction. Another method is to ask the player to replay his positioning. Inevitably, players get lower when asked to replicate the position than they did initially. By demonstrating the difference between their perception and the reality, players understand better and can make a better effort to correct the position. Video is an effective teaching tool because it eliminates language's ambiguity.

Teach with cue words, not lengthy explanations

After players understand the basics, use cue words rather than lengthy instructions. Do not overwhelm players. If players hear only negative explanations or corrections, confidence suffers. Also, if a coach, trainer or parent corrects every mistake, the coach talks for the entire practice rather than the player shooting. Some frequent cue words I use:

- *Small to tall*: Catch the ball low in a crouched position and finish the shot fully extended from the toes through the fingers.
- *Reach to the rim*: Some players actually shoot too high, with their follow-through almost vertical. Instead, reach to the rim at the end of the follow-through to ensure there is horizontal force; the angle of release should be around 55-degrees, not 90-degrees.
- *Finish the shot*: The most common refrain when players miss short is "follow-through." However, the problem is often not the hand's follow-through, but the body's finish. Many players never fully extend their hips.
- *Shoot out of a telephone booth*: Shoot up, then out. Some players extend their elbow before their shoulder rotates, creating a flat shot.
- *Strong at the finish*: Some players snap their wrist back when they release the ball, rather than holding their follow-through. I want players to be strong and balanced when they finish their shot.
- *Toe to the target*: Many players never square all the way to the basket, and it starts with their footwork. If the shooting toe points to the target, the body follows.
- *Straight through the ball*: Once the player gets aligned properly, if his or her arm and hand move in a straight line during the shot, the ball goes straight.
- *Index finger to the center of the rim*: Rather than "reaching into the cookie jar" or a "goose's head" finish, I prefer a relaxed finish with the index finger pointing at the rim. Essentially, the wrist

moves through 180-degrees of motion, starting with the wrist extended so the back of the hand is parallel to the floor and finishing with wrist flexed and palm parallel to the floor.
- *Early*: Too many players shoot after gravity takes over and deceleration begins. Shoot early in the shot to utilize the full force from the lower body.
- *Don't Squish the Worm*: Keep the ball in the fingers, not the palm of the hand.

Part II: Shooting Progression

6

Phase I: **Stationary Shooting**

In Phase 1, I concentrate on technique. In the initial form shooting drills, there is no shot preparation. In a sense, a form shooting drill is one which excludes the shot preparation.

Players often start the shot pocket around their hips in the triple threat position. I teach the triple threat differently and consequently have a different shot pocket. The common triple threat position negates its desired affect, which is a player who is ready to pass, dribble or shoot. I use the *Hard2Guard position*: the ball is cocked in front of the player's armpit ready to shoot. The player is positioned to make a push pass, extend with the dribble or rotate quickly into a shot or shot fake.

Hard2Guard Position

- Athletic stance with knees over toes and shoulders over knees and shooting foot forward
- Eyes soft centered on the rim to allow peripheral vision to see the entire scoring zone
- Ball cocked: wrist is extended so there is a "wrinkle in the wrist"
- Ball positioned in front of the armpit with elbow close to the body
- Protect the ball against tight defense by remaining active with fakes and pivots

The difference between the more common triple threat and the Hard2Guard position is subtle. The Hard2Guard position develops an attacking mindset and encourages players to make plays, while the triple threat is a defensive position concerned with ball protection. Players who use the triple threat start their shot pocket at their hip and dip the ball when they receive a pass, even when they catch and shoot. They develop the habit through thousands of shots originating at the hip. The Hard2Guard position's higher shot pocket eliminates the dipping habit.

If the player takes the ball off the catch or off the dribble and gets the ball to the shot pocket with his body squared with the shooting foot, elbow, hand and ball aligned, he increases his success and establishes the proper starting position. If something is amiss during the shot preparation, and balance and alignment in an athletic stance are not attained, the shot mechanics must compensate for the error, which changes the shot. The mechanics receive the bulk of the instructional emphasis, but the shot preparation determines success. Successful shot preparation ensures the same mechanics on every shot.

During this first stage of learning, stay close to the basket and limit movement. As one demonstrates more and more consistency - not just success, but technique consistency - add distance and variables. Makes and misses mislead players, especially novices. Developing consistency supersedes making shots initially. Makes increase confidence, but if the player sacrifices his technique to make shots, which is common among young players, the initial success leads to poorly developed habits and stalled development. Focus on technique, not the outcome of the shot, and develop consistency before adding distance or variables.

In Phase 1, I limit players to form shooting, free throws (or an approximation of a free throw if a player cannot shoot from 15 feet with proper technique) and catch-and-shoot shots.

Form shooting is controlled, with the player taking his time to concentrate on the proper technique close to the basket without movement. Form shooting ignores the shot preparation and focuses solely on the mechanics, from the set point (Hard2Guard position) to the finish. Players take their time to balance in an athletic stance, fine center on the target, line up the shot line with the rim, and find the correct hand placement. Use form shooting to automate this position and train the shot's extension and finish. When initiating a form shooting drill, start without the ball. Move through the shot mechanics without the ball and concentrate on the feel of the shot. Retrace the shot from the finish to the set point and try again. Once the player is ready to use the ball, have the player shoot, hold the finish until the ball hits the net and re-trace his steps from the finish to the set position. Place the ball in his hands to prevent dipping the ball or a lower starting point. The speed of execution is unimportant early in the learning process: work on the body position, extension and finish on the form shots to build good habits. Free throws are a specific form of form shooting.

Catch-and-shoot shots add speed, movement and soft to fine centering through the addition of two variables: (1) receiving the pass and going directly into the shot; and (2) basic step-in footwork. When receiving the pass:

- call for the ball with the palm of your shooting hand; fingers point to the sky
- receive the ball at the depth of the shot, knees bent and hips down to facilitate a quicker shot

The movement and speed on catch-and-shoot shots is restricted to one step. With body square to the basket, start in a staggered stance with knees bent and hips down. As the pass is made, step into the shot with the back foot (the right foot in the picture on next page) and keep the front foot planted. For a right-handed shooter, his right foot always remains slightly forward of his left foot in a shooter's stance. When the left foot is the pivot foot (pictured next page) step in with the right foot slightly ahead of the pivot foot. When the right foot is the pivot foot, take half a step with the left foot, stubbing the left foot to keep the right foot forward in the shooting stance. As the ball hits the hands, the step should hit the ground. Stay low on the step to the basket to keep the hips loaded. The shoulders stay over the knees and knees over the toes. The tendency is to stand when stepping in to the shot, which extends the hips and decreases the power. The quick step facilitates an efficient and quick shot, provided the body remains at the base of the shot on the reception of the pass.

On the change from a form shot to a catch-and-shoot shot, the eyes shift focus. During form shooting, the player has time to fix his eyes on the target. However, on the catch-and-shoot, the player must watch the pass into his hands and quickly sight his target.

While these changes from form shooting to catch-and-shoot shots seem simple, do not underestimate the subtle changes and their affect on the shooting process. Form shooting is a warm-up exercise to teach the proper set position, extension and finish, but the shots are not game quality. Catch-and-shoot shots resemble the static nature of form shots, but add more variables which add a more game-like shooting quality.

When teaching the step-in on the catch-and-shoot shots, practice using both feet as the plant foot. I favor the inside foot one-two-step as the dominant method of footwork, especially when shooting. Some coaches teach a permanent pivot foot and others teach a jump stop, and neither is incorrect. However, especially with young players, I favor the inside foot for three reasons:

1. Young players need to develop both feet just as they develop both hands.
2. The inside foot offers a consistent motion into the shot regardless of which direction the player moves.
3. The one-two-step offers a greater impulse – force reduction over a longer period of time – which assists with the acquisition of balance.

At this stage, players stand as the pass is made and take one step into the catch with the other foot planted. Use each foot as the plant foot to prepare players for the next step – movement – which requires players to use both feet equally. Build good habits with the shooting technique to provide a good foundation for future shooting success. Catch-and-shoot shots are among the most frequent game shots, so there is no need to rush through this phase.

Phase 1 Matrix

1 – *Mistakes include*: lack of balance in a stationary position – weight not evenly displaced between both feet and/or inability to squat into an athletic stance with shoulders over knees and knees over toes; poor coordination between upper and lower body; the ball starts too low or the player starts his shooting motion from the left to middle of his body (for a right-handed shooter) rather than in alignment; incorrect hand placement; shoots flat-footed; low follow-through; hand never completely under the ball resulting in more of a push than a shot; follow-through to the side; and/or thumb the ball with the non-shooting hand or shoots a two-handed shot.

2 – Starts in an athletic position with shoulders over knees and knees over toes; and correct hand placement with the index finger and middle finger centered on the ball. *Mistakes include*: steps-in too far with his shooting foot so he shoots with a staggered stance and poor balance; poor coordination between upper and lower body; the ball starts too low or the player starts his shooting motion from the left to middle of his body (for a right-handed shooter) rather than in alignment; shoots flat-footed; low follow-through; hand never completely under the ball resulting in more of a push than a shot; follow-through to the side; and/or thumb the ball with the non-shooting hand.

3 – Step-in to a shooter's stance with shooting foot slightly forward; weight evenly displaced between both feet; athletic stance with hips back and knees over toes; and follow-through straight to the rim. *Mistakes include*: stands upright on the step-in; turns body on the step-in; the ball starts too low or the player starts his shooting motion from the left to middle of his body (for a right-handed shooter) rather than in alignment; incomplete extension of the ankle or hip; low follow-through; and/or thumb the ball with the non-shooting hand.

4 – Step-in to a shooter's stance with shooting foot slightly forward and body directed at the target; weight evenly displaced between both feet; athletic stance with hips back and knees over toes; ball starts from the set position with hand under the ball and alignment of the ball, hand, elbow and foot; and follow-through straight to the rim. *Mistakes include*: stands upright on the step-in; incomplete extension of the ankle or hip; low follow-through; and/or slight interference from the non-shooting hand.

5 – Step-in to a shooter's stance with shooting foot slightly forward; maintain the flexed position on the step-in; weight evenly displaced between both feet; athletic stance with hips back and knees over toes; full extension of the ankle, knee and hip; ball starts from the set position with hand under the ball and alignment of the ball, hand, elbow and foot; high follow-through with hand pushing all the way up and through the ball; follow-through straight to the rim; and no interference from the non-shooting hand which falls off the ball as the shooting hand starts its follow-through.

Free Throws

Free throws are a special shot because of the mental aspect. On any court, in any situation, a free throw is the exact same shot: one shooter, no defense and the basket 10-feet in the air, 15-feet away. Whether shooting in one's driveway or in front of 25,000 screaming fans, the shot is the same. The only difference is the impact of the game, fans and pressure on one's mind. The goal is to overcome the mind block which prevents the shooter from feeling comfortable. As Gonzaga University's Assistant Coach Jerry Krause says, "Like eating, you shouldn't have to think about shooting free throws."

Players struggle from the free throw line for three reasons:

1. Skill
2. Approach
3. Attention

Players like Shaq have sub-par shooting skills which hinder their free throw performance. Chapters 2 and 6 cover the specifics of the shooting technique. Very few players – even those who we consider to be good shooters – have technically perfect shots. The players who do – Jason Kapono, Steve Nash, Jose Calderon, Ray Allen, etc. – are the ones who shoot 90+% from the free throw line every year. Those in the 70-80% range often have slight technical deficiencies which lead to inaccuracies. They shoot well because they shoot so many shots and their shots are highly repeatable, but the slight flaws contribute to missed shots.

Beyond the skill of shooting, many players miss because of their approach. The approach encompasses three things: (1) practice approach; (2) mental approach; and (3) physical approach.

Practice Approach

Everyone has a different free throw practice philosophy, but I don't know that any method has proven successful. Practicing free throws is different than shooting in a game. The difference is mental. Coaches tire out players before practicing free throws or attach a consequence to a missed free throw, but these approaches fail to help a player make free throws in the game because neither approach attacks the true issue. Players may miss because they are fatigued, but is the miss because they are too tired to shoot the free throw correctly or because the fatigue affects their approach? If they are able to make a jump shot during the flow of the game, is fatigue really the issue at the free throw line?

When I was a college assistant coach, the head coach gathered the staff together to plan the next part of practice while the players shot free throws. In this environment, players go through the motions: they reinforce the same habits. Once a player's shot is automated, he needs deliberate practice to improve. Deliberate practice requires a specific goal, immediate feedback and player concentration. When players shoot on their own, they fail to create a specific goal and they lack the concentration required to improve.

Typical free throw practice is to shoot free throws over and over to master the distance and the shot. Several studies suggest that variable training improves performance better than the typical block practice. In one example, 8-year-olds tossed beanbags to targets. One group practiced tossing to targets 2-feet away and 4-feet away, while the other group tossed only to targets 3-feet away. When they tested the subjects at a later date, the subjects who tossed to variable targets performed better at a test at 3-feet than did those who practiced at 3-feet (Schmidt).

"This result suggests that learning how to modulate the relationships among the target distances was more important for a test at any one target than was specific experience, even at the particular target distance used at test," (Schmidt). This study suggests that players should practice their free throws from random distances, not just 15-feet.

When I coached a women's team in Sweden, we spent 10 minutes every day on form shooting and free throws. We started in front of the rim. Players made three in a row and then they took a step back. If they missed, they started at the beginning. The goal was to make 15 shots in a row. Players took shots from variable distances rather than shooting from one distance.

"Variable practice alters the practice context to force a change in behavior from trial to trial, encouraging additional information processing activities about the lawful relationships among the task variants. The result is learning that contributes to performance on the test of retention or generalizability, even though these activities detract from momentary performance during the acquisition phase," (Schmidt).

Changing the distance between repetitions helps players develop into better shooters. While shooting from variable distances might not help you make 15 shots in a row, it helps your subsequent performance in a game. The point of practice is to improve game performance, not to enhance practice performance. Transfer to the game is the determining factor of the practice's effectiveness.

Mental Approach

Players who shoot high percentages embrace free throws; players who struggle fear free throws. Many players concentrate on the wrong thought: "I hope I don't miss." Furthermore, because we remember images and emotions, we remember the agonizing miss more than the make. "When we make a four-foot putt, there may be some relief but usually not a lot of emotion. However, when we miss a four-foot putt, there is often a reaction of frustration or anger. That emotional reaction imprints more strongly in our memory, which means the image of missing is more likely to come to mind when we encounter a similar four-footer. That undermines our confidence and we're more likely to miss," (Parent).

When we make a free throw, there is relief, as everyone expects to make a free throw. However, when we miss, we grow frustrated. If I make nine free throws in ten attempts during a game, but the one miss could have sealed a victory, I remember the miss because of the emotional reaction. Next time, I hope to avoid the same situation, rather than feeling confident because I shot 90%. The emotional miss changes my mental approach.

Successful players, and successful shooters, are not always the best physical performers. They are the players most equipped to deal with situations. We remember Michael Jordan for all his game-winning shots, but he missed more than he made. However, he never allowed the misses to affect his confidence and he prepared to make the next shot when he got another chance.

Rather than reacting emotionally to a missed free throw, notice the result and move forward. Once a shot misses, you cannot change the result. You can only make the next play. By managing failures, you are more confident in the same situation during the next game.

Physical Approach

A routine (below) is a positive physical approach which can enhance one's free throw performance. However, many players do something while standing at the free throw line which negatively affects their performance. Some players stare at the basket for several seconds; some freeze in the middle of their shooting rhythm; some start their shot from the left side of their body;

some bend their knees to different depths each time. To shoot a high percentage, you need to eliminate things that can go wrong. Many players bend their knees to initiate their shooting motion; however, when they are fatigued, they forget to bend or their knee bend is inconsistent. I encourage players to set before their routine so they bend to a consistent depth each time. They consciously bend their knees before starting their routine rather than incorporating their knee bend into their subconscious shooting technique. I also want the last action of their routine – the last dribble, spinning the ball – to be with their shooting hand so they bring their off-hand to the ball, rather than bringing their shooting hand across their body to the ball. By correcting these minor physical mistakes, players eliminate many mistakes, which give them a better chance to make the shot.

Players miss free throws because they have lazy or bad habits. I attended the 2008 NCAA Tournament West Regional and watched specific shooters at the free throw line. Texas A&M's James Jones comes set with the ball in the middle of his body with his right (shooting) hand on the side of the ball. He circles the ball to the left as he brings it to his shot pocket. As he shoots, his hand never reaches a consistent position at the release because of the circling motion. Sometimes he follows through straight to the basket, but often times his follow-through is off to the right, following the circular motion. If he concentrated on the pick up of the ball and his hand placement, he would improve his shooting percentage.

Marquette's Dominic James shot like he had a sprained right ankle. His entire body leaned to the left. He subconsciously shifted his weight off his injured leg. My guess is a lingering right ankle sprain or a bad habit which developed when he had a sprained ankle. Either way, a good shooter misses because he leans left during his shot.

The key to 90% free throw shooting is eliminating possible mistakes. Everyone misses occasionally due to lack of concentration, fatigue, etc. However, to shoot 90%, you need to eliminate the other mistakes. When you lean to one side or circle the ball into the shot, you add variables which lead to mistakes and fewer made shots. In the tournament when games are close and every shot counts, these bad or lazy habits can decide the outcome of a game.

Attention

As players learn to shoot free throws, they need to direct their attention appropriately. In games, free throws often occur after an emotional experience – a hard foul, a missed shot, late game, etc. As a player approaches the free throw line, he needs to focus his attention. If he thinks about the missed shot, the hard foul, the next play, the last time he missed a free throw or anything else, his thoughts contribute to sub-optimal shooting performance. Coaches and parents exacerbate the situation by yelling at the player, so his attention shifts from his target to the instruction: he thinks his way through his shot (often second-guessing himself) rather than shooting subconsciously.

To improve, he needs to quiet his mind. One strategy is to create a trigger word and concentrate on the word. The goal is to stop the internal dialogue and focus on the shot using a narrow-external mode of attention, allowing your body to move without over-thinking the process. When he thinks about a previous shot or his coach's advice, he loses his focus on the shot.

These three things – skill, approach and attention – work together and complement each other. When a player develops the proper technique, his confidence improves and he has the right mental approach. The right skill and mental approach leads to the player directing his attention properly. When a player approaches the free throw with confidence and a consistent approach; quiets his mind and focuses on the task; and shoots with good technique, he shoots successfully.

Routine

Players use a routine to build consistency, comfort and confidence at the free throw line. "Employing a rigid pre-shot routine will help you master your free throw, according to a study in the *Journal of Sports Sciences*." The routine calms the player and reminds the body of the hundreds of similar shots one has practiced. The familiarity builds confidence and dispels pressure. Pressure or stress results from a disparity between the task and one's perceived ability. The routine relaxes a player because he realizes he has made this shot a thousand times.

To maximize the routine, use these nine steps:

1. Receive the ball off the free throw line. Relax: 10 seconds is a long time.
2. Take a deep breath in through the nose and exhale slowly. This helps slow your breathing and your heart rate. Pressure situations can "shut down the capillaries in your fingertips, causing a loss of fine motor control," which affects one's shooting. To combat these "adrenaline bombs," the Navy Seals take several deep breaths to flood their body with oxygen before doing something which requires fine motor control, like de-activating a bomb (Drury). To shoot better under pressure, players do not need more practice. Instead, they need to learn how to handle pressure.
3. Close your eyes and visualize your made free throw. Mental imagery increases relaxation, builds confidence and imprints a fresh vision of a made free throw. "You have a short term visual memory, and if you shoot with the image of a missed shot in your mind, then your eyes will naturally tend to focus on where your last shot hit the rim instead of correctly on the center point of the basket. The image of the missed shot also reinforces a negative expectation rather than a positive expectation of the ball going through the hoop," (Mikes).
4. Step to the free throw line; find the nail on the floor and line up your shot line with the nail (center of the rim). Your shot line is your set point, not just your shooting toe. If your set point is inside your shooting toe, as in my example in the section on Alignment, adjust your stance accordingly so the set point is centered toward your target.
5. Bend your knees to the depth of your shot and do your routine. The actual routine, to me, is of little consequence provided you follow the other steps and the routine is the same every time you shoot a free throw.
6. Finish the routine with the ball in your shooting hand. Many right-handed players dribble with their left hand or spin the ball with their left hand and bring their right hand across their body to put their shooting hand on the ball. Always finish with the shooting hand on the shooting side of the body and bring the off-hand to the ball. Maintain the alignment of the shooting hand.
7. Come to a set position and inhale. At the set position, the wrist should be cocked and the fingers should point to the sky. Many shooters have their fingers across the ball, which is poor shot preparation. When shooters set, they should be aligned to the basket, including the hand and fingers, like the Hard2Guard position.
8. Fine center on the target.
9. Exhale and shoot.

In the far left, a picture of a proper set position for a free throw. Some prefer a higher set point on a free throw, like in the Hard2Guard position, but this is another option. In the middle picture and below, the shooting hand placement is across the ball, rather than fingers pointing to the rim, as in the picture on the left. As you can see, my elbow is already starting to point outward. The incorrect hand placement, common on free throws when players dribble with their left hand and bring the right hand to the ball creates a poor shooting position.

7

Phase II: **Movement**

Phase 2 introduces movement and shooting footwork. When people think about footwork, they picture jump stops and pivots and post moves. Footwork is more than the actual steps, but how the player uses each step. Proper foot placement and weight distribution create more effective moves and eliminate extra steps or inefficient movements which result from a subtle lack of balance or lack of acceleration when the foot placement or weight distribution is off.

Footwork is the economy of motion and involves the proper weight distribution to maintain balance and increase acceleration. Players with great footwork use their foot placement to enhance their moves. A player's anticipation enhances his footwork.

Shooting-specific footwork involves two types of stops: the 1-2-step and the Jump Stop. These stops differ from the lunge stop and hockey stop, which are general methods of deceleration. Instead, these methods finish with players in a proper shooting position.

- **1-2-step**: a step-step stop finishing in a shooting stance.
- **Jump stop**: hop off one foot and land on two feet.

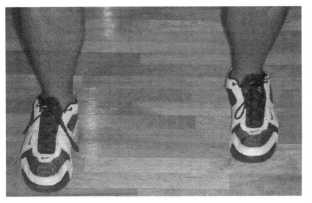

When players stop, their feet should be in a heel-toe relationship with the shooting foot slightly forward (left). Rather than stop one's momentum with the long final step – like the lunge stop – players using the 1-2-step must drop their hips when decelerating.

The jump stop differs from the hockey stop because the shoulders stay square and the player does not lean into a jump stop. Instead, he drops his hips to stop forward momentum. Imagine the butt as the anchor; if you drop your butt, you can stop on balance.

When a player stops in a more upright position, he tends to turn his foot as a braking mechanism, like a hockey stop. When he turns his foot, he turns his body away from the basket, facing the side of the backboard or even the baseline corner. When he stops with a staggered stance or opens his body too much, he no longer is positioned to shoot. While deceleration is overlooked as the cause of shooting mistakes, if a player does not acquire balance during his shot preparation, his technique will be off.

The proper foot placement and weight distribution impact the player's balance as he begins his shooting technique. As players incorporate movement into their shooting, start with straight-ahead movement to limit the variables. The player starts facing the basket and moves in a straight-line to the basket, receiving the pass from under the basket. These are not the most game-like shots, but the player must develop general footwork and balance before moving to more game-specific shooting drills.

As the player receives the pass, his weight should be distributed evenly between his two feet and he should be in a crouched position with his knees over his toes and shoulders over his knees. Before starting his shooting technique, he should establish a *zero point of momentum*: all forward momentum stops. As he improves, this stop is imperceptible, as he transitions from running forward to jumping in a split-second. However, if the player does not decelerate completely before starting his shot, his balance will be affected and he will have to account for his momentum while in the air. Players like Kobe Bryant have an amazing ability to attain balance while in the air; however, young players need to acquire balance on the ground before trying to emulate one of the greatest athletes in the world.

Because shooting requires a change from horizontal to vertical movement, if the player fails to acquire balance, he drifts in the direction of his horizontal movement: when running straight ahead, he continues straight ahead. To improve results, drop the hips, with head over the lower body base of support to stop momentum and shoot in one plane.

Emphasize the inside foot 1-2-step

There are three methods of basketball footwork: jump stop, inside foot and permanent pivot foot. None is incorrect.

- **Permanent pivot foot**: the player pivots with the same foot every time; a right-handed player uses his left foot as his pivot foot, regardless of the situation.
- **Inside pivot foot**: the player pivots on his inside pivot foot every time; players use both feet as their pivot foot, which creates consistent body movement on each side of the court.
- **Jump stop**: the player hops off one foot and lands on two feet together – if he catches with his feet in the air, the player can use either foot as a pivot.

I teach the inside foot 1-2-step. A player cannot always choose his pivot foot, so he must be able to use either foot. I ran a workout for a talented AAU team that taught a permanent pivot foot. We played 1v1, with the offensive player cutting to get open. Several times, right-handed players received the pass with their right foot as their pivot foot, and they traveled because they were unaccustomed to using their right foot.

I want players to use the inside foot 1-2-step to develop both feet, like using either hand for a lay-up. When I allowed some players to use their preferred footwork, they developed and relied on bad habits. The 1-2-step provides a longer impulse to apply force over a greater amount of time, resulting in better balance without sacrificing quickness. For older or more advanced players, we train the 1-2-step and the jump stop because the jump stop is appropriate in some situations, like receiving a pass against pressure. On some dribble moves, especially inside the key, we use a jump stop, but in the shooting zone, I teach an inside foot 1-2-step. I use the 1-2-step exclusively in the learning progression because I think it develops the best habits and the most consistency.

1-2-Step Checklist

- Use the inside foot
- Anticipate the stop on the first step of the 1-2-step to slow one's momentum
- Ensure the first step hits the ground as the ball is received and the second step follows quickly
- Catch at the depth of the shot with feet slightly wider than shoulder width
- Prepare for the shot before receiving the pass with hands ready to catch and shoot. Know where your defender is upon reception, so you know if you are open
- Eliminate dipping the ball; use the Hard2Gurd position as the shot pocket

The inside foot 1-2-step is quicker than the permanent pivot foot when going to the left for a right-handed shooter or right for a left-handed shooter. When using the outside foot as the pivot foot, the player cannot aggressively step in to the catch. He steps around the catch with a reverse pivot on his permanent pivot foot. The step-in to the catch provides a better rhythm for the shot, as the player moves to the basket, rather than making a slight reverse pivot.

The jump stop affords the same advantages as the inside foot, but many players have lazy feet: they receive the pass with one foot on the ground and then hop into the jump stop. While most officials ignore it, if a player then uses a pivot foot, it is a traveling violation. I also dislike the jump stop, especially for younger players, because they land in a more upright position, making it tougher to decelerate completely, which causes them to drift on their shot.

The jump stop is effective when the player has time to prepare to stop or is at less than full speed. When using a jump stop, players struggle to stop momentum completely. Stopping momentum is easier when moving in a straight line to the basket, rather than at an angle.

1-2-Step Advantages

- Consistency of motion compared to the permanent pivot foot
- Quicker than a permanent pivot
- Better balance than a jump stop
- Quicker stop off the dribble than a jump stop

Linear, then Lateral

The Phase 2 progression starts with straight-ahead movement and progresses to moving at an angle. Initially, start with the body square to the basket and move in a straight line. I start in the center; however, you can use five or seven spots around the floor (below) to work on all angles, but move in a straight line to the basket from each spot.

As the player cuts to the ball, he should be in an athletic position. He must move quickly to receive the pass, but when the ball is in the air, he must anticipate the stop and drop his hips. If he waits until he receives the pass to initiate the deceleration, he will not have time to stop in a good shooting position. Two techniques one can incorporate on the initial step of his 1-2-step are (1) taking a long step or (2) stepping heel-to-toe. To step in left-right, his long step and/or the heel-toe step occur with his left foot. The long step and the heel-to-toe step create a negative shin angle which initiates the player's deceleration. If his body weight is forward of his foot on the foot strike, as in a normal stride pattern, he cannot stop in a shooting stance.

As he approaches the pass, he shows a target with his shooting hand calling for the ball. Once he shows the target, his body should be in a crouched position. As he receives the pass, his first step of his 1-2-step hits the ground. In the stationary catch-and-shoot shots, the player planted one foot and stepped into shooting position with the second foot. On the move, only the timing differs. Rather than planting one foot, the first step hits as he catches, and the second step follows closely. When a right-handed player steps into his shot left-right, his foot pattern is normal; however, when he steps in right-left, he stubs his left foot to keep his right foot forward in a good shooting stance.

After players learn to stop and shoot off a straight-line cut, move to lateral motion. Everything stays the same, but the player pivots slightly on the catch to square to the basket. I start with curls from elbow to the elbow because: (1) the elbow gives players a consistent distance to increase consistency and confidence; (2) players receive the pass moving to the basket, if they use an inside foot 1-2-step; and (3) it limits the speed initially.

When curling, point the toe of the initial step toward the target and step in with the second step. For a right-handed shooter curling from the right elbow to the left elbow, point the right toe toward the basket and stub the left foot so the right foot remains forward. When receiving the pass on the curl, there are three foot placements to get the right foot pointed at the rim: (1) step with an outside-in motion on the right foot; as the foot rolls into a flat position, the foot turns toward the basket; (2) step to the catch and then pivot slightly on the ball of the foot as the left foot steps-in to the shot; or (3) catch heel-to-toe on the right foot, so the foot has an extra beat to rotate to the basket. Pointing the right toe at the rim opens the hips, which quickens the step-in and creates the desired alignment, as the body follows the foot.

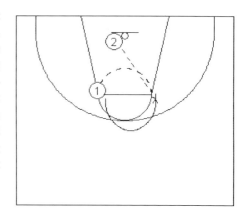

When moving from the left elbow to the right elbow (right), the initial step is with the left foot. However, the important step, for a right-handed shooter, is the second step with the right foot. Often, the player either under-rotates to get the shot off more quickly or over-rotates. Under-rotation is when he shoots with his left foot forward and never squares to the basket. Over-rotation is when the right foot steps too far, so his body turns toward the left side of the backboard rather than to the rim. Point the right foot to the target to create the desired alignment of the shooting foot, elbow, hand and ball.

Refine Technique

While the basic technique remains the same, the shot's feeling differs. The first difference is maintaining balance in the air: if the player fails to stop on balance before jumping, he or she drifts or turns in the air. Next, the player must learn when to release the ball. For most players, this differs based on the shot's location. In the paint, release the ball at the top of your jump, as the height of the release is more important than the power because of the defender's proximity and the shot's distance. At the three-point line, release the ball early in your jump to utilize the lower body power; the height of release is not as important, as few players shoot contested threes. Players need time to develop the feel of these different shots. Often the close range shots present more problems, as players judge the release point poorly and shoot a flat shot rather than maintaining the same technique with a high release.

Shot reminders

- Shoot in one motion
- Shoot early in the jump
- Shoot with the legs
- Stay square to the target throughout the shot

Phase 2 Matrix

1 – *Mistakes include*: catch off-balance; over-square on the step-in, so body is not directed at the target; step-in too erect; fall forward, backward or sideways on the shot; twist in the shot; incomplete extension – hips stay flexed and you lean forward on the shot; dip the ball at the catch; set position in the middle of your body or the left side – no alignment before the shot; shoot too late in the jump; shoot left to right; low follow-through – push the ball to the basket; and/or snap your hand back at the release.

2 – Catch on-balance; and shoot in one plane – no forward, backward or sideways movement. *Mistakes include*: over-square on the step-in, so body is not directed at the target; step-in too erect; incomplete extension – hips stay flexed and you lean forward on the shot; dip the ball at the catch; set position in the middle of your body or the left side – no alignment before the shot; shoot too late in the jump; low follow-through – push the ball to the basket; and/or snap your hand back at the release.

3 – Catch on-balance in a crouched position and step-in to the shot with body squared to the basket and shooting foot slightly forward; catch at the depth of your shot; and shoot in one plane – no forward, backward or sideways movement. *Mistakes include*: step-in too erect; incomplete extension – hips stay flexed and you lean forward on the shot; dip the ball at the catch; set position in the middle of your body or the left side – no alignment before the shot; shoot too late in the jump; low follow-through – push the ball to the basket; and/or snap your hand back at the release.

4 – Catch on-balance in a crouched position and step-in to the shot with body squared to the basket and shooting foot slightly forward; complete ankle, knee and hip extension; catch and move the ball to the set position with hand under the ball and elbow under your hand; catch at the depth of your shot; shoot in one plane – no forward, backward or sideways movement; high follow-through. *Mistakes include*: dip the ball at the catch; shoot too late in the jump; and/or snap your hand back at the release.

5 – Catch on-balance in a crouched position and step-in to the shot with body squared to the basket and shooting foot slightly forward; catch at the depth of your shot – no dip; catch and move the ball to the set position with hand under the ball and elbow under your hand; complete ankle, knee and hip extension; shoot on the way up; shoot in one plane – no forward, backward or sideways movement; high follow-through; and strong at the finish – hold the follow-through.

8

Phase III: **The Bounce**

Shooting off the dribble is similar to shooting on the move. The only difference in the shot preparation is the difference between moving the ball from the catch to the shot pocket and moving the ball from the dribble to the shot pocket. A right-handed player shooting off a right-handed dribble pounds the ball into his right hand and brings the off-hand to the ball. When shooting off a left-handed dribble, he sweeps the ball from the reception of the dribble with his left hand to his right hand, eliminating any sideways movement by the shooting hand. The right hand waits, cocked and ready with fingers to the sky, for the left hand to sweep the ball into place to maintain alignment.

Emphasize footwork

Footwork entails more than the pivot foot or the method of stopping (jump stop vs. 1-2-step). Footwork involves establishing balance and positioning the player in an offensive position. One problem is the inability to decelerate in a parallel stance (shooting stance). Players are unable to slow their momentum to control their center of gravity. They never establish balance, take extra steps and/or hop. If they use a 1-2-step, they combine the lunge stop and the hockey stop: they finish in a staggered stance, but the front foot is angled away from the basket, turning their hips.

When shooting off the dribble, the player should use a 1-2-step. To prepare for the shot, he must anticipate the stop and use a low, hard last dribble to get his legs underneath the shot and enable him to jump straight up. On his initial step of the 1-2-step, he points his toe to the basket to square his body. When his second foot strikes, he is ready to shoot with his feet in a "heel-toe" relationship with the shooting foot forward. If he dribbles right, a right-handed shooter continues in normal stride with a left-right 1-2-step; if dribbling left, he stubs his left foot, so the right foot remains the front foot.

I worked with a player this summer whose father advocated an open stance for shooting and believed his son used this open stance. However, when he shot a free throw, he shot with a parallel stance. When I watched him shoot on the move, his "open stance" resulted from an inability to decelerate, as he used a hybrid lunge/hockey stop, with a staggered stance and feet, hips and shoulders pointed away from the target. He had almost no bend in his knees or flexion in his hips and could not shoot accurately when moving quickly before the shot. He used the turn as a breaking mechanism, which created the open stance. Once he learned to decelerate by bending his knees and dropping his hips, he did not shoot with an open stance and his accuracy improved.

Prepare for the shot. Two techniques to incorporate are (1) taking a long step or (2) stepping heel-to-toe. Each method occurs on the first step of the 1-2-step: if the player drives to the right, he stops left-right, so the long step or the heel-to-toe step is with his left foot. The long step and the heel-to-toe step create a negative shin angle which initiates the player's deceleration (bend the knee to prevent hyperextension). In either case, the player must sit his hips lower into this step. As his right foot steps into the shooting stance, his momentum stops and he is on balance and prepared to shoot.

Because balance is so important, work on straight-ahead drives before angled drives. Once players establish balance and a solid base moving toward the basket, attack from an angle, which increases the footwork demands. Limit variables in the learning process. Adding the dribble is one variable, so restrict the motion, to focus on the pick up of the dribble and the footwork. Once players are comfortable shooting off the dribble in a straight line, incorporate angled drives.

When attacking at an angle, many players never fully square to the basket or they square too far. Some fail to establish balance and drift in the direction of the drive. In most cases, poor footwork causes these issues. When driving at an angle, the player uses the first step of the 1-2-step to turn to the basket. Pointing the toe to the target opens the hips, which enables a quicker pivot to the basket and establishes the base: if the base is square to the basket, the rest of the body squares to the basket. As I once heard: "If you start in the correct position and finish in the correct position, everything in between takes care of itself."

Ball handling

Ball handling and shooting are viewed as separate skills though enhancing one's ball handling control improves shooting percentages, especially off the dribble. Ball handling is part of the shot preparation, as the pick up of the dribble initiates the shot. If a player has better control with the ball, he can move from the reception of the dribble to the shot more quickly and with better hand positioning. When the ball gets into the player's palm and wrist, showing a lack of ball control, the player has more difficulty positioning his hand and getting into his shot quickly. When shooting off a move, many shots miss because of the reception of the dribble, which affects the shot. A great ball handler can use the dribble to enhance the rhythm of his shot, not detract from it. To help increase a shooter's proficiency off the dribble, work on ball handling control drills to improve the pick up of the ball. I started my "If you can dodge a wrench" series to improve this aspect of shooting.

Vary the speed of attack

Different attacks provide different challenges, as a full court pull-up differs from a one-dribble pull-up. I start with a two-dribble pull-up. Full court pull-ups challenge deceleration, balance and shooting technique, while one-dribble pull-ups challenge footwork. The two-dribble pull-up provides enough speed to train deceleration and balance, as well as training the footwork and pick up of the dribble. Once players master the basics through the two-dribble pull-up, add the one-dribble pull-up and the full court pull-up.

The two-dribble pull-up provides a good tempo and rhythm. Start about 25-feet from the basket and attack straight ahead with the dribble to shoot from just inside the free throw line. Initially, use the players preferred footwork – a right-handed shooter steps into the shot with a left-right step-in. Next, move to a right-left step-in.

If players struggle to stop with their feet pointed to the basket with their 1-2-step, use the right-left step-in (for a right-handed shooter). For some players, this footwork forces them to stop their momentum on the first step (right foot) because they have to stub the second step (left foot). They learn to anticipate the stop on the first step. With the preferred footwork (left-right), players often rely on the final step with the right foot to decelerate, which causes them to turn their right foot to the side to stop their momentum, leaving them in a poor shooting position.

After players get comfortable shooting off the dribble with the two-dribble pull-up, incorporate full court pull-ups and one-dribble pull-up jump shots. Some players excel at the full court pull-up jump shot, while others avoid it. When players practice a full speed, full court pull-up jump shot, they typically slow down over several steps. I trained a player who constantly missed short of her shots. When we watched her on video, we saw that she leaned back in an effort to decelerate rather than sitting her hips down in an athletic stance. By leaning back, she eliminated much of her vertical push.

To attack and decelerate quickly, the player must anticipate the stop and sit his butt down (drop his anchor). I worked with another player, and in a shooting drill where he ran from half-court to shoot at the free throw line, he actually started his deceleration at the mid-point between half-court and the free throw line. Rather than sprint and "stop on a dime," he slowed down into his shot because he played the game too upright in his stance which did not provide the strength to stop his forward momentum quickly.

The challenge is acquiring balance and not allowing the horizontal momentum to affect the shooting technique. Often, the player does not stop his forward momentum before leaving the ground, and he leans forward as he shoots. Players also tend to jump higher to try and balance in the air when shooting a full court pull-up jump shot. When they release the ball from a higher point, due to the jump, they tend to shoot the ball flat. As they jump, players must shoot the ball up and then out to be successful. Even at the faster speed, they want to shoot the same shot as with the two-dribble pull-up, and this puts an even greater emphasis on the stop to reach a zero-point of momentum.

The one-dribble pull-up often feels unnatural, especially when attacking toward the pivot foot with a crossover step.

- **Direct drive**: (right) attack in the direction of the lead foot. With a left-foot pivot foot, the first step is with the right foot and the direction of the drive is to the right, with a right-hand dribble. The right foot step and the dribble hit the ground simultaneously to avoid a traveling violation.

- **Crossover drive**: (left) attack in the direction of the pivot foot with the lead foot "crossing over." With a left-foot pivot, the first step is with the right foot and the direction of the drive is to the left with a left-hand dribble.

On a direct drive, the rhythm and feel is similar to a two-dribble pull-up. The player uses three steps and drives at the basket. On a one-dribble pull-up with a crossover drive, the player uses only two steps, meaning the first step of his attack is also the first step of his 1-2-step. This feels awkward for most players because the first step must be long and quick, but the player also must anticipate his stop on this step. However, this guarantees an inside foot 1-2-step. For a direct drive with a left-foot pivot, the footwork is right-left-right with a right-hand dribble. However, for a crossover drive with a left-foot pivot, the footwork is right-left with a left-hand dribble.

Players feel a lack of separation on the crossover drive and hop into a jump stop. This is not wrong, but, depending on the situation, it is less efficient. If the player needs to create more space from his defender, and chooses not to use a second dribble, a jump stop is appropriate if it creates separation. When attacking the front of a zone defense, a player could use a jump stop to split the top defenders, rather than dribbling again and risking a steal. However, for most one-dribble pull-ups, separation is not an issue because the initial defender is out of the play, and the help defender is too far away to contest the shot. The one-dribble pull-up is not a move that is always available, but it is a frequent shot.

General to Specific

After mastering the general off the dribble shots, incorporate different cuts into shooting off the dribble. Make a cut, receive the pass, shot fake and make a quick one or two-dribble direct or crossover drive into a shot. Start with catching while moving straight to the basket and progress to making a move off a curl cut.

Players are most open when they first receive a pass. Therefore, offensive moves start with a catch-and-shoot and progress from there. The next progression is to catch, shot fake and go. Many coaches and players start from the jab step. Starting with the jab step assumes that players catch the ball with a defender present. In the scoring zone, most players receive a pass because the passer felt they were open. They may not have space to shoot an uncontested shot, but the defender is not set in his defensive position. The shot fake is the next progression because it draws the defense toward the offensive player, and the defender usually raises his center of gravity, giving the offensive player the opportunity to attack. Also, when a player squares for a shot or shot fake, he maintains court vision; when a player jab steps, he often drops his eyes. Therefore, starting with the catch-and-shoot and moving to the shot fake enhances the player's ability to find an open teammate and encourages players to attack rather than waiting for the defense to set.

Phase 3 Matrix

1 –*Mistakes include*: off-balance; never fully control momentum; shoot with the non-shooting foot forward or step-in too far with the shooting foot and shoot with a staggered stance; turn your body rather than staying square to the basket; for a right-handed shooter, off a left-hand dribble, bring the right hand to the ball; off a right-hand dribble, bring the ball to the middle of your body to meet your left hand; fall in the direction of the pre-shot movement; shoot with two hands – shooting hand never gets under the ball; shoot left to right; incomplete extension – shoulders stay forward and there is a forward lean in the torso; shoot late in the jump; low follow-through – push the ball at the basket; and/or snap your hand back at the release.

2 – Stop on-balance; and get the ball to the set position with your hand under the ball and elbow under your hand. *Mistakes include*: shoot with the non-shooting foot forward or step-in too far with the shooting foot and shoot with a staggered stance; never fully control momentum; turn your body rather than staying square to the basket; fall in the direction of the pre-shot movement; incomplete extension – shoulders stay forward and there is a forward lean in the torso; off a left-hand dribble, bring the right hand to the ball; for a right-handed shooter, off a right-hand dribble, bring the ball to the middle of your body to meet your left hand; shoot left to right; shoot late in the jump; low follow-through – push the ball at the basket; thumb the ball with the non-shooting hand; and/or snap your hand back at the release.

3 – Stop on-balance with body square to the basket in an athletic stance with shooting foot slightly forward; get the ball to the set position with your hand under the ball and elbow under your hand; and shoot in one plane – no forward, backward or sideways movement. *Mistakes include*: for a right-handed shooter, off a left-hand dribble, bring the right hand to the ball; off a right-hand dribble, bring the ball to the middle of your body to meet your left hand; shoot left to right; incomplete extension – shoulders stay forward and there is a forward lean in the torso; shoot late in the jump; low follow-through – push the ball at the basket; and/or snap your hand back at the release.

4 – Stop on-balance with body square to the basket in an athletic stance with shooting foot slightly forward; get the ball to the set position with your hand under the ball and elbow under your hand; complete ankle, knee and hip extension; shoot in one plane – no forward, backward or sideways movement; high follow-through; and strong at the finish – hold the follow-through. *Mistakes include*: for a right-handed shooter, off a left-hand dribble, bring the right hand to the ball; off a right-hand dribble, bring the ball to the middle of your body to meet your left hand; shoot left to right; and/or shoot late in the jump.

5 – Stop on-balance with body square to the basket in an athletic stance with shooting foot slightly forward; off a right-hand dribble, pick-up the dribble with the right hand and bring the left hand to the ball (for a right-handed shooter); off a left-handed dribble, pick-up the dribble with the left hand and sweep the ball across to the right hand; get the ball to the set position with your hand under the ball and elbow under your hand; complete ankle, knee and hip extension; shoot in one plane – no forward, backward or sideways movement; shoot on the way up; high follow-through; and strong at the finish – hold the follow-through.

9

Phase IV: **Game Movement**

The fourth phase involves shooting in a game context: going from general shooting lessons to specific shooting success. By developing good habits initially, the progression to game shooting builds seamlessly. A player with good technique who can establish balance when moving quickly with or without the dribble in any direction is prepared to shoot game shots. Players struggling with the general shots because of their technique or balance or deceleration must address their flaws before shooting more specific or difficult shots.

A good shooter prepares mentally and physically to shoot before he receives the pass. Mentally, he anticipates the openness of the shot.

- How close is my defender?
- How quick is my defender?
- Does he or she gamble?

When using a screen, he makes this decision in a split second with the ball in the air. If a player intends to shoot, he must catch the ball ready to shoot, which requires preparing mentally and anticipating the shot.

Physically, he receives the pass in shooting position: an athletic stance or a crouched position. In shooting drills, a player can run upright around a chair, catch and shoot because the drill lacks a game's intensity, speed or defense. In a game, a defender will fight through the screen if the shooter runs upright. In every drill, practice good, game-like habits. Practice makes permanent.

Players must be in an athletic position when they make contact with their screener. Getting low is not an action completed on the last step before the catch. Players must run in a low position, ready to catch and shoot at any time.

When the ball is in the air, the player must prepare mentally to step in to the pass and decelerate with the first step of his 1-2-step. When a player learns the hockey stop, he anticipates and leans into the stop; if he fails to anticipate and create a wide base, he sways: his upper body continues moving in the direction he was going while his lower body changes directions.

If the player does not anticipate the 1-2-step and decelerate on his first step, he travels, uses a lunge stop, or uses a combination hockey stop/lunge stop. None is a good option. The lunge stop leaves the player with a staggered stance, with weight on the forward leg (second step), while the combination lunge/hockey stop leaves the player with his lead foot, hips and shoulders turned away from the target.

To improve balance when receiving the pass, anticipate the stop. When a player cannot anticipate because the pass is thrown too early or the defender is in position to steal the ball, he is not likely to catch and shoot. It happens; some cuts, some passes and some plays are not conducive to a cut, catch and shoot, and the offensive player must make the decision whether he is open or not. If he is racing his defender to the ball, he is not open for a shot; secure the pass first and make a move accordingly, maybe a crossover drive one-dribble pull-up. In instances when the player judges himself to be open to catch and shoot, he must anticipate the stop on the first step to improve his footwork and create a balanced position.

Use of screens

As players master their shooting technique and move to more difficult shots, getting open becomes part of the shot preparation. Players must know how to separate from the defense with and without the ball, while using a screen and without one. A friend told me about a high school coach in Texas who spoke to the coaches association about zone offense. As he was announced and walked to the podium, the other coaches prepared to scribble notes. He stepped to the podium and said his zone offense was based around one concept: "Go where they ain't." He thanked the audience and returned to his seat.

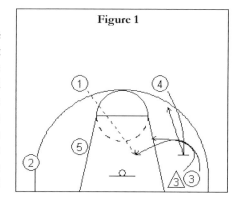

In some ways, basketball is really that simple. When getting open, the golden rule is to move as far from the defender as possible. A coach can teach multiple rules for each situation, but when making a split-second decision, thinking about which rule to follow slows down a player. "Going where they ain't" uses a player's common sense, as he reacts to the defender's decision and moves away.

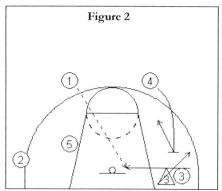

While this is the golden rule, players should learn some specifics. A few instructions:

- If the defender trails, curl (Figure 1)
- If the defender shoots the gap, cut backdoor (Figure 2)
- If the defender goes under the screen, fade (Figure 3)
- If the defender fights through, make a straight cut (Figure 4)

The curl cut is preferred because it takes the player toward the ball and the basket. The straight cut starts as a curl; if the defense takes away the curl, the offensive player cuts away from the defender using a straight cut.

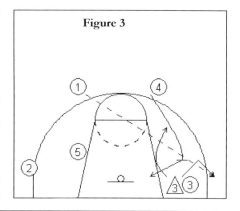

How does a shooter read his defender? First, players are creatures of habit, so defenders often defend a screen the same way the entire game. After a few possessions, the offense anticipates the defense. Second, the shooter must see his defender. Coaches teach offensive players to go "shoulder to shoulder" with the screener. I teach the shooter to touch the screener's hip, cutting off the defender's path as with the "shoulder to shoulder" instruction.

As the shooter touches the screener, he looks down his inside arm to see his defender. He reads his defender and decides to curl or fade. If he fades, he pushes his screener into his defender's path. If he cannot touch the screener because his defender is there, he cuts backdoor. He touches the screener's hip to remind himself to get low in a crouched position, ready to catch and shoot as soon as he hits the screen. Finally, I use the "hand to the hip," rather than "shoulder to shoulder" because the game is physical and the shooter must protect his space, fight off his defender and not allow the defender to force him wide to create space to slip through the screen.

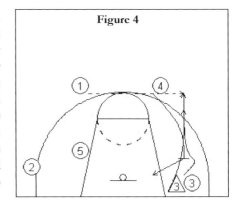

Figure 4

Flare Screens

While I use general shots to develop confidence and technique, many game shots occur when receiving a pass while moving away from the basket. As the progression moves from form shooting to movement to dribbling to game shooting, the technique remains constant. The shot preparation, the deceleration and the attainment of balance differ.

This section covers two types of shot preparation: (1) running away from the basket, like on a screen the screener play; or (2) moving away from the basket at an angle, like off a flare screen out of a 1-4 high set.

Screen the Screener

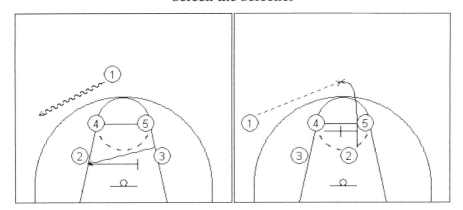

The Screen the Screener play, also called "America's Play," can be run out of numerous sets; in this case, a box set. As the 1 dribbles to the side, 2 screens for 3. 4 and 5 set a double screen for 2 who receives the pass for the shot. Notice the hook at the end of the cut on the right.

1-4 High Flare

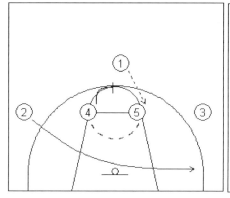 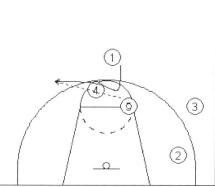

In this play, the 1 enters the ball to the 5 in the high post. The 2 clears a side and the 4 sets a high flare screen for the 1. The 1 uses the screen and catches the skip pass for a shot.

Shooting when running away from the basket

If the player feels his defender or sees his defender's hand in the passing lane, his focus changes from shot preparation to catching the pass. The defender's proximity changes the play, the mindset and the footwork. The receiver runs to the catch to cut off the defender's angle, squaring shoulders to the catch or catching with his outside hand to use the width of his body to protect the ball.

When the offensive player is open or feels daylight between him and his defender, he catches intending to shoot. Shooting off a straight cut away from the basket, like in the screen-the-screener play, requires a 180-degree pivot to the basket. On the initial step of the 1-2-step (inside foot), the player throws his leg to the ball. He *hooks* to the ball: the final two steps make the rounded end of a hook. Throwing the leg to the ball cuts the angle of his pivot. By stepping to the ball (rather than continuing in a straight line), the pivot is more like a quarter turn.

The foot placement is the same as a curl, as the player can: (1) step with an outside-in motion on the initial step; as the foot rolls into a flat position, the foot turns toward the basket; (2) step to the catch and then pivot slightly on the ball of the foot as the second foot steps in to the shot; or (3) catch heel-toe on the initial step (right), so the foot has an extra beat to rotate to the basket. Pointing the toe at the basket opens the hips, which enables a quicker pivot, and creates the desired alignment.

The step to the catch was difficult to capture, but I tried. In this case, the pass is made from the wing, where the picture was taken. As I approach the top of the key, I step all the way to the ball, a quarter turn and use the heel-toe footwork. As I receive the ball, I would pivot and step my right foot into my shooting position.

To review:

- Run to the spot
- Decide if open while the ball is in the air
- If open, hook to the ball on the 1-2-step

- Square body to the basket in a crouched position
- Shoot

Flaring off a screen

Shooting off the angle, like off a flare screen, is easier in terms of squaring to the basket. There are two basic flare screens and the footwork differs slightly for each: (1) when the cut starts with the back to the basket, like flaring off a down screen (Figure 5); and (2) when the cut starts with the player facing the basket, like a flare screen out of the 1-4. The second difference is the distance the player must cover, as there are two basic types of footwork: (1) crossover step or (2) backpedal.

Flare from a down screen

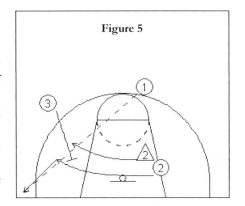

Figure 5

1. Cut to the screen
2. Make contact with the screen
3. See the defender go underneath the screen. By underneath, the defender goes to the ball side of the screener.
4. If backpedaling, push-off with the inside foot and square shoulders to the passer
5. If using a crossover step, step across with the inside foot and keep hips open to the passer
6. Move below the level of the screen: create the most distance from the defensive player

Use the first five steps when facing the basket and flaring from a high screen. With a high screen, move above the level of the screen to maximize the distance.

Another variation of the flare off a high screen occurs if the point guard passes to the wing and makes a UCLA-cut. On the UCLA-cut, the point guard cuts off a high screen from a post and cuts to the block; if the defender quickly takes away the basket cut, he can take the defender below the screen and pop back behind the screen and away from the defender. The Utah Jazz's Deron Williams often uses this maneuver.

The high flare screen is used most commonly out of a 1-4 set when the pass is made to the high post and the other post sets the flare screen. This is the easiest shot off a flare cut, as the body is square and the shooter can backpedal. Backpedal when covering only a couple feet. When backpedaling, stride rather than taking baby steps. When backpedaling off a cut initiated when facing the basket, the hips are open to the basket; catch in a crouched position with weight on the balls of your feet in an athletic position and shoot. Some players backpedal in an erect position, which leads to negative momentum on the shot. Sit the hips down with shoulders over the knees and knees over the toes. Using a high flare screen is like using any other screen; be prepared to catch and shoot.

When backpedaling off a down screen, the player must maintain the crouched position. He should hit the screen in a low, crouched position. On his final step, as he receives the pass, he pivots to the basket. Because a flare cut often requires an overhead pass, the pass is often high and the shooter must reach for the pass and land in a crouched shooting position ready to shoot.

On the crossover step, the player hits the screen and uses a crossover step to separate from the screen, while keeping hips open to the passer. A crossover step is like carioca, except the trail leg never goes behind. When moving from left to right with a crossover step, step the left foot in front of the right foot, then the right foot steps, then the left foot steps in front, etc. Use 3-4 steps total on the crossover step, which should cover 10 or more feet.

When flaring, the player looks over his inside shoulder in a crouched position. As the ball approaches, he turns to receive the pass with his body square to the basket. There is often time to separate from the screen and turn before the pass arrives. If not, he receives the pass and then squares to the basket. Flaring off a down screen and fading to the corner is more difficult than flaring off a high post screen because of the body's angle at the reception. On a fade to the corner, the final step is a quarter turn to square to the basket. Again, the key is to square on the catch and stop all negative momentum before starting the shot.

Game-specific Drills

As players automate the full spectrum of shots, increase the drills' game-like quality: increase the drill's intensity and specificity and incorporate defense. As intensity increases, volume decreases: intensity and repetitions are inversely related. If a player makes 10 shots in a ¾ speed warm-up drill, make five shots in a full speed, game-like shooting drill with a longer break in between repetitions. Use a player's offensive system to create game-like drills: practice shots he shoots in a game.

Add distance, creativity and intensity

Coaches frequently criticize players' habits because players only want to shoot three-pointers or make fancy dribble moves, while coaches want players to be disciplined and play hard. Shooting three-pointers, making fancy moves or going hard is not the problem. The problem occurs when players and coaches are unwilling to progress gradually. Impatience is a problem, as everyone wants to be good right away. Anyone can shoot; this progression develops makers, the elusive 180 Shooter.

What is a player's range? A player's shooting range is the distance he or she can shoot without sacrificing his technique. Once his technique changes and he pushes the ball or throws the ball at the basket, he is too far. A player's range may differ from his or her scoring zone. In general, the scoring zone starts a large step behind the three-point line and moves to the basket: this is the area a defender must honor an offensive player's scoring ability.

An individual's scoring zone is the area in which a player can score effectively. Effective is a vague term and can be clarified by age and a specific coach. An individual's scoring zone is the area in which he or she has a green light to shoot if open. A player may have the technique to shoot three-pointers, but not the accuracy, so his or her scoring zone does not extend as far as his or her range. Miami's Dwyane Wade, for example, has three-point shooting range, but he is not an accurate three-point shooter, so his scoring zone is inside 20 feet.

For varsity players, I suggest a player shoot 70+% in practice from a spot for it to be considered his scoring zone. One cannot shoot 40% from the three-point line in practice and expect to shoot 40% in games. *Shooting 40% in a gym without defense is not making shots; it is missing shots.*

In practice, train general shots to build confidence and refine technique and incorporate shots that challenge the player and elicit improvement. If a player is successful at one shot, and only practices the one shot, he will not improve. A player must leave his comfort zone. In general, I spend 70-80% of training on previously mastered shots and 20-30% challenging the player through a higher intensity or greater distance. With the previously mastered shots, I add repetitions to train conditioning or lower repetitions to train speed or make the drill more competitive. When moving outside the individual's comfort zone, I replace conditioning, intensity and competitiveness with a more positive environment, more time and more teaching. Often, we use the same general drills, but extend the range or add an element.

Beyond distance, challenge the player's comfort zone through creativity. Many players lack creativity. However, the best players are creative in their training. An average shooter shoots during training; a great shooter imagines the shot in a game context, hears the crowd, sees his defender, feels his uniform and smells the sweat. This visualization and creativity enhance his training and its transfer to a real game situation.

I assisted with a shooting camp for college players. The players varied from walk-ons to high major starters. After watching some general shooting drills, the high major Division I player stood out, and it had nothing to do with his shooting success. Instead, the biggest difference was his ability to make a drill game-like. The players shot off the dribble, which for the majority meant taking one to two dribbles and shooting. However, the high major DI player looked like he was playing 1v1 against an imaginary defender. He started from a triple threat position with jab steps and sweeps; his body position on the drive was low and aggressive; he changed speeds; no two repetitions looked the same: his shots differed from a hard pull-up, to a freeze jump shot, to a step-back. He got something out of the drill. He had a mental plan and used his imagination to turn a simple drill into valuable shooting practice.

Phase 4 Matrix

1 – *Mistakes include*: travel on the catch while turning toward the basket; catch off-balance; fall backward or sideways on the shot; over or under square, so body is not directed at the target; lean back on the catch which prevents full hip extension; dip the ball at the catch; set position in the middle of your body or the left side – no alignment before the shot; twist in the shot; shoot too late in the jump; shoot left to right; low follow-through – push the ball to the basket; and/or snap your hand back at the release.

2 – Catch on-balance with a 1-2-step, and pivot without traveling; and shoot in one plane – no forward, backward or sideways movement. *Mistakes include*: over or under-square on the step-in, so body is not directed at the target; lean back on the catch which prevents full hip extension; dip the ball at the catch; set position in the middle of your body or the left side – no alignment before the shot; shoot too late in the jump; low follow-through – push the ball to the basket; and/or snap your hand back at the release.

3 – Catch on-balance with body square to the basket and shooting foot slightly forward; catch at the depth of your shot; and shoot in one plane – no forward, backward or sideways movement. *Mistakes include*: catch too erect; dip the ball at the catch; set position in the middle of your body or the left side – no alignment before the shot; incomplete extension – hips stay flexed and you lean forward on the shot; shoot too late in the jump; low follow-through – push the ball to the basket; and/or snap your hand back at the release.

4 – Catch on-balance in a crouched position with body square to the basket and shooting foot slightly forward; catch and move the ball to the set position with hand under the ball and elbow under your hand; catch at the depth of your shot; complete ankle, knee and hip extension; shoot in one plane – no forward, backward or sideways movement on the shot; high follow-through. *Mistakes include*: dip the ball at the catch; shoot too late in the jump; and/or snap your hand back at the release.

5 – Catch on-balance in a crouched position with body square to the basket and shooting foot slightly forward; catch and move the ball to the set position with hand under the ball and elbow under your hand; catch at the depth of your shot – no dip; complete ankle, knee and hip extension; shoot in one plane – no forward, backward or sideways movement; shoot early in your jump; shoot on the way up; high follow-through; and strong at the finish – hold the follow-through.

10

Phase V: **Pro Shots**

By the fifth phase, a player's shot is autonomous; he has mastered his technique and shooting is a subconscious skill, like riding a bike. At this point, incorporate higher levels of intensity and conditioning, as executing under pressure and fatigue increases his success.

The previous chapter described the difference between the practice habits of good players and a high major Division I starter who used his creativity and visualization to make his practice more valuable. When I train players, I see a four-step progression:

- **Imitation**: Players follow directions and try not to mess up the drill (ex: where do I go after I make the shot? Which hand do I dribble with?)
- **Action**: Players do the drill and concentrate on the skill involved (ex: How do I make a hesitation move?)
- **Comprehension**: Players think about the action and how it might work in a game (How can I beat a defender with the hesitation move?)
- **Individuality**: Players imagine a game situation and make the drill personal through visualization (This time, I'm going to hesitate like I am pulling the ball out to run a set and when my defender relaxes, I'm going to explode by him.)

Players rarely express this difference and many do not realize the transformation. However, when I see a player using his imagination, rather than doing the drill, I know he is ready to perform. The differences are subtle, and many may not notice, as in each case, the player does the same thing (ex: a hesitation move and a lay-up). The differences matter: doing a drill is different than training for game performance; drills cannot replicate the game situation and merely train the technique. Using one's technique in a game situation is a skill, and using the imagination and visualization trains the skill, not just the technique. As the player moves from Action to Comprehension and Individuality, the technical skill incorporates a tactical component, and the tactical component gives the skill a game-like quality, which makes the move more realistic and enhances the transfer from training to a game.

> **Technique**: the closed-skill mechanics.
>
> **Skill**: the open-skill execution of a technique with its perceptual, decision-making and contextual elements.

When players use their own creativity, they take ownership of the drills and moves. They train for themselves, not for me or anyone else. They no longer practice my moves, but train their own. My goal is not to create copycats, but to assist players with skill development. Teaching players to use their imagination and creativity is a very real aspect of the learning process.

By this point, a player's shot is automatic. If he shoots poorly, he needs to re-learn his technique. Players who shoot well proceed. Coaches use reduced feedback and teach more through questions. When I train a player individually, I ask him where he gets the ball, how his coach uses him, where he gets his shots, how defenders play him and more. I use general shots and shots common to multiple offenses to structure his practice around the types of shots that he shoots and the scenarios that he faces.

With my own team, I use more specific shots, as I know the answers. I use more specific questions for each player:

- How are they playing you when you use this screen in this set?
- Where are you open to shoot?
- What can you do to get open when the PG drives?

I use the questions to start the thinking process:

- During this set, I want you to imagine the way he played you last game and make a different move each time for a 15-foot pull-up jumper.
- During this set, we are going 1-4 low at the end of the quarter with nine seconds to go. Get your shot.
- During this set, you have an aggressive defender trailing you on the screen. Mix up your shots each time.

Rather than tell the player the answer, I evaluate the player's thought process. If he does the same thing over and over again, he fails to utilize his imagination. Something does not make sense. Either he does not understand my instructions or he has a poor feel for the defense. If I discover the reason, we can make progress. Learning that the player has a poor feel for the defense explains his underperformance in games. If this is the issue, we use video of previous games and illustrate the opponent's defense. If he does not understand my instructions, I must improve my communication, by re-phrasing the instruction, providing a better demonstration or giving the player more time to process the instructions on his own.

Use defense in shooting drills

Game shots are rarely wide open. As players reach this phase, the tactical elements are as important as the technical elements. If a player cannot get open for a shot, is he really a great shooter?

Instituting defense is risky, as you do not want a player to land on a defender's foot and twist his ankle. Artificial defenders, in my opinion, cause more injuries than a live defender. Therefore, I use live defenders (these serve as my breakdown defensive drills, too).

In the first defensive progression, I tell the shooter where the defense will be. For instance, I instruct the defense to trail the cutter around the screen. The shooter knows beforehand which cut to make, eliminating any decision-making process, and he anticipates a contested shot after the cut. The defense is present to disrupt the shot, not to block it or play full speed.

After several repetitions, I change the drill, so the offense has one open shot and one contested shot in a set. For instance, the shooter curls off an imaginary down screen to the right elbow and shoots. After the shot, he cuts through and curls off his partner, who sets a screen on the left side. The shooter curls off this screen toward the left elbow. As soon as the shooter passes his screen, the screener turns and chases the shooter. If the shooter does not catch and shoot, they play 1v1 from the catch.

In the second progression, I create an artificial situation: the player knows he will be open when he receives the pass, but the defense plays freely. For example, we play 1v1 with the defense starting on the midline and the shooter on the wing at the three-point line. On the skip pass, the shooter is open with the defender closing out. The defender is free to play the situation any way he wants, but he starts in a disadvantaged position so the shooter is open.

In the next progression, we play 2v2 live where the ball handler's goal is to draw two and kick. In addition to a penetration-and-pitch drill, it is also a help-and-recover defensive drill. With only two defenders, there is room to find space for an open shot, but the defense is live, forcing players to move and react with a game-like quality.

These three progressions with a live defender ensure a lot of shots, rather than relying on 5v5 scrimmages for contested shots or completely artificial defense, as with a partner shooting drill with a pass and a closeout. These drills bridge the gap between training the shooting technique and making shots during games.

The Step-Back

A step-back move is a way to create space for a shot when tightly defended. Many players prefer the step-back move, especially for a right-handed player dribbling left. These players step in to their shot with a right-hand dribble and a comfortable left-right step-in, but when dribbling left, they use the step-back rather than a right-left step-in. The step-back is a useful move, but it should not be used too often, as it is a contested, off the dribble jump shot, which is a fairly low-percentage shot. However, in late clock situations or when a team needs its go-to guy to create a shot, the move is useful to have at one's disposal.

A "step-back" jump shot is a misnomer. In truth, the player neither "steps" nor moves directly backward. The two keys to a step-back move are:

(1) The move originates on the inside foot – the foot toward the defender

(2) The player moves in the shape of a "V."

The inside foot creates a stronger push and pushes the defender on his heels, making the step-back more effective. The harder the defender works, or the faster he moves, the less space the offensive player must create, as the step-back works against the defender's momentum.

Stepping back in the shape of a "V" creates more space. When a player steps directly backward in relation to the basket, he creates less separation and a more difficult shot. The defense closes out in a straight line, making it easier to contest the shot, and there is no rhythm. In some cases, as with the San Antonio Spurs' Manu Ginobili, it works, but using the V-shaped step-back (moving back and to the side) creates a more open, more rhythmic shot.

As a player attacks from the right wing toward the middle of the floor, he steps into the defender with his right foot and hops off his right foot. However, he continues toward the middle of the floor, creating the V-shape and separating from the defender. He turns his body while in the air so he lands with his body squared to the basket. The jump is quick with feet close to the ground.

Some teach a true "step-back," where the player steps back with his left foot, lands and pivots to the basket while he steps with his right foot into shooting position. Like the jump stop vs. the 1-2-step, this is not incorrect. However, the one-count is quicker in this instance, establishes a more balanced position than the quick pivot and is less likely to draw a whistle from an official for a traveling violation.

From a live ball move, the offensive player must sell the first step forward to get the defender on his heels, and then create sufficient space with the step backward.

From a live ball move (Hard2Guard position), the player makes an aggressive dribble to put the defender on his heels. The dribble must sell a drive and force the defender to retreat. Then, he plants on his inside foot and hops back and away to create space. If using the step-back while dribbling, the step-back move works against the defender's momentum, as he cannot react quickly enough to contest the shot. The faster the ball handler drives, the less space he has to create with his move because the defender's momentum does most of the work.

A defender has one last gasp if beaten: swiping at the ball. If the ball is exposed, which is common when transferring the ball from a left-hand dribble to a right-handed shot, the defender can deflect the ball. Keep the ball tight to the body on the transfer from the left to the right hand. If the ball separates from the body while the player squares to the basket, the defense can swipe at the ball and create a turnover or disrupt the shot. Keep the ball tight to the body to protect it.

To teach the step-back move, I start at the free throw line and set up a chair and a cone in the "V" shape. The chair gives the player an initial target, signifying the defender reacting to his first step. The cone gives him a target, as he lands behind the cone.

I start with one step; if a player can make the one step move from a Hard2Guard position, he can make the move off the dribble. The one-step move simplifies the footwork and limits the variables, but it is a tougher shot against a defender because there is less speed to use against the defender.

Starting in the Hard2Guard position, the player makes a crossover step (step with the right foot across the body) to step into the defender (chair) and then hops and lands behind the cone. As he lands, he bends his knees and drops his hips to stop, land on balance and power the shot. The step-back move is not a fade away; once he lands, all movement is up and to the basket. The shot technique never changes.

The step-back move is an advanced shot and some players may not be able to utilize this move. Players who push the ball or use their arms to compensate for the lack of forward momentum need to start closer to the basket. However, it is easier than some assume. The step-back move is like using a jump stop, except the jump stop moves away from the basket in the shape of a V.

To review:
- Start on the inside foot
- Hop back in the shape of a V
- Square to the basket on the hop
- Keep feet close to the ground
- Land on-balance at the depth of the shot
- Bring the off-hand to the ball to pick up the dribble
- Shoot with the legs
- Shoot a regular jump shot, straight up and down

One-foot Step-Back

I call the one-foot step-back the "Steve Nash Step-Back." The one-foot step-back starts the same as a step-back – the player pushes away from the defender with his inside foot and turns his body in the air. However, rather than land with a 1-2-step or a jump stop, the player lands on his outside foot and jumps off the one-foot to shoot. The motion is like the *Ice Skater Drill*. This creates a harder shot, as it is more difficult to land on one foot, establish balance and jump to shoot than it is off a two-foot landing. I use this move as a teaching tool to train balance, footwork and body positioning. If the player can establish balance and the proper body position off one-foot, his regular two-foot step-back move will be more explosive.

Freeze J

The freeze jump shot is a variation of an off the dribble pull-up jump shot frequently used by Chauncey Billups, Kobe Bryant and others. The freeze J is almost the opposite of a hesitation move: a hesitation move is used to fake a shot and explode past the defender; the freeze J fakes a drive to shoot over a retreating defender.

The freeze J fakes acceleration to the basket, so the move starts with a slower dribble. I start players walking toward the basket in a crouched position as if approaching a defender. As they take their last dribble, they take a long, quick step, like a drive step. Then, they step in with their other foot and shoot rather than taking a full stride to the basket.

The freeze J requires a little rhythm and coordination. The difficulty, for most players, is that a right hand dribble requires a right-left step-in. As the player walks toward his defender, he fakes the drive with a hard step on his right foot, steps with his left foot into shooting position and shoots. A left-hand dribble leads to a left-foot drive step, so the player steps in to his shot left-right.

Because the step fakes a drive step, the player cannot step directly at the defender (depending on distance, this is possible on some occasions). If the defender is within range of the shooter, he fakes a drive past the defender. The first step is the fake. As he steps with his second foot, he pivots and squares his body to the basket.

Other than the footwork, the freeze J is the same as a normal pull-up jump shot. Because of the fake drive to the basket, the body is in a low, crouched position and the speed is minimal. After mastering the coordination and the pivot to square to the basket, the freeze J is just another pull-up jump shot variation.

Because the freeze J fakes the acceleration to the basket, it can also be used after a hesitation move. The player sprints toward the basket, hesitates and then uses the fake drive step to push the defender back on his heels before rising for a jump shot. Start with a slow dribble and the freeze J first, and once the player builds comfort with the move and its footwork, use the move off the hesitation dribble to add another weapon.

Spin Shot

The spin shot series builds upon a spin lay-up and a spin dribble. Kobe Bryant, Kevin Garnett, Steve Nash and others use the spin shot and fake spin shot to create space for mid-range jump shots.

Players should use a spin or fake spin only against body contact from the defender. When dribbling with his right hand, the player feels the defender on his left hip, plants his left (inside) foot and lowers his body posture. With his left foot planted, he reverse pivots, turning his back to the defender. The ball remains in his right hand as he pivots and pulls the ball to his right shoulder. He steps away from the defense with his right foot, picks up the ball with two hands and moves it into shooting position. He steps with his left foot into shooting position and shoots.

Fake Spin Shot

When the player dribbles with his right hand and feels the defender on his left hip, he plants his left (inside) foot and lowers his body posture. With his left foot planted, he makes a quarter-turn reverse pivot and turns his back to the defender. The ball remains in his right hand as he pivots and he uses his head and shoulders to sell the pivot. Then, he makes a quarter-turn front pivot, steps into his shooting position and shoots.

Final Thoughts

- Practice makes Permanent
- Learn proper shooting mechanics before working on full speed shooting drills.
- The shot preparation is as important as the shot mechanics.
- Practice game shots at game speeds from game spots.
- Learn body awareness so one can self-correct.
- Track Progress religiously. Every shot counts.
- Practice with a partner.
- Shooter's Mentality: Stay Positive, Catch in Position to Score, Think Shot Every Time, Anticipate before Reception, Sprint the Floor, Use Screens Properly, Stay in Motion.
- BELIEF: Balance, Eyes, Line, Index Finger, Extend, Follow-Through
- The Three C's: Concentration, Confidence and Consistency
- Basketball is a mental game; practice mental skills.

Phase 5 Matrix

1 – *Mistakes include*: off-balance; no deceleration; never fully control momentum; turn body rather than staying square to the basket; travel on the stop; shoot with the non-shooting foot forward or step-in too far with the shooting foot and shoot with a staggered stance; fall in the direction of the pre-shot movement; for a right-handed shooter, off a left-hand dribble, bring the right hand to the ball; off a right-hand dribble, bring the ball to the middle of your body to meet your left hand; shoot with two hands – shooting hand never gets under the ball; incomplete extension – shoulders stay forward and there is a forward lean in the torso; shoot late in the jump; shoot left to right; low follow-through – push the ball at the basket; and/or snap your hand back at release.

2 – Stop on-balance; and get the ball to the set position with your hand under the ball and elbow under your hand. *Mistakes include*: never fully control momentum; turn body rather than staying square to the basket; shoot with the non-shooting foot forward or step-in too far with the shooting foot and shoot with a staggered stance; fall in the direction of the pre-shot movement; for a right-handed shooter, off a left-hand dribble, bring the right hand to the ball; off a right-hand dribble, bring the ball to the middle of your body to meet your left hand; incomplete extension; insufficient leg drive; shoot left to right; shoot late in the jump; low follow-through – push the ball at the basket; thumb the ball with the non-shooting hand; and/or snap your hand back at release.

3 – Stop on-balance with body square to the basket in an athletic stance with shooting foot slightly forward; get the ball to the set position with your hand under the ball and elbow under your hand; and shoot in one plane – no forward, backward or sideways movement. *Mistakes include*: for a right-handed shooter, off a left-hand dribble, bring the right hand to the ball; off a right-hand dribble,

bring the ball to the middle of your body to meet your left hand; incomplete extension; shoot late in the jump; shoot left to right; low follow-through – push the ball at the basket; and/or snap your hand back at release.

4 – Stop on-balance with body square to the basket in an athletic stance with shooting foot slightly forward; get the ball to the set position with your hand under the ball and elbow under your hand; complete ankle, knee and hip extension; shoot in one plane – no forward, backward or sideways movement; high follow-through; and strong at the finish – hold the follow-through. *Mistakes include*: for a right-handed shooter, off a left-hand dribble, bring the right hand to the ball; off a right-hand dribble, bring the ball to the middle of your body to meet your left hand; shoot left to right; and/or shoot late in the jump.

5 – Stop on-balance with body square to the basket in an athletic stance with shooting foot slightly forward; off a right-hand dribble, pick-up the dribble with the right hand and bring the left hand to the ball (for a right-handed shooter); off a left-handed dribble, pick-up the dribble with the left hand and sweep the ball across to the right hand; get the ball to the set position with your hand under the ball and elbow under your hand; complete ankle, knee and hip extension; shoot in one plane – no forward, backward or sideways movement; shoot on the way up; high follow-through; and strong at the finish – hold the follow-through.

Part III: Extra Shooting

Appendix I:
Common Shooting Flaws

While every player's shot is unique, a few flaws consistently plague shooters and result in poor technique and shooting percentages.

Be Early, Not Late

When shooting a jump shot, shoot early in the jump to maximize the leg drive. A common instruction is to "wait until the top of the jump." At the top of the jump, the body decelerates; thus, the shot derives less power from the legs and more from the upper body, which applies a horizontal force. When shooting close to the basket, as with a post player or a dribble pull-up in the lane, shooting at the top of the jump creates a higher release point enabling the offensive player to shoot over a defender. However, from three-point-range, shoot early in the jump to power the ball up and to the basket.

Set Position

The set position is about eye level, just off the shooting eye (left). Some shoot slightly higher or lower. However, those who shoot from a drastically different position reduce success. Some players shoot across their body (a right-handed shooter with a set position on the left side of the body), a habit born when they were young and weak and shot three-pointers; they have the cross body motion which helped them propel the ball to the basket. Some shoot on top of their head, where their arm motion is not an extension, but a slinging motion to the basket, creating a very flat, very hard shot. Some dip their shooting shoulder to power the ball, almost like a shot put motion. And, some shoot too far off their shooting eye, forcing the mind to unconsciously determine the correct line of flight for the ball, as it is a different angle than the line of sight.

Correct these flaws through proper alignment. The line runs from just inside the shooting toe through the shooting knee to the elbow, hand and ball. Deviation from this line impacts the shot.

Narrow Stance

As with a building's foundation, the base must be solid or it may be compromised. Players who shoot with narrow feet (less than shoulder width apart) are more likely to sway, jump to the side, lean or fall backward; in other words, they have difficulty stopping their momentum and remaining balanced throughout the shot. They lack balance at the transition from shot preparation to technique and are more likely to miss (picture right).

Flat-footed

Some players shoot flat-footed, especially from the free throw line. On a shot, the first motion in the link is a forceful ankle extension; the heel rises off the ground as the body extends. Players who shoot flat-footed miss this initial extension and the antagonist muscles of the lower body work to keep the ankle dorsiflexed, inhibiting some power application from the lower body. In affect, the body works against itself.

Dipsy-do

The shot preparation is not an aid to power the ball. During the shot preparation, bend your knees to the depth of the shot. No downward motion occurs during the shooting technique. Every movement is an extension up and to the basket until the final wrist flexion. Any added flexion in the knees or hips is inefficient and slows the shot.

Hand Placement

Incorrect hand placement leads to numerous flaws, from incorrect follow-through to pushing the elbow out of alignment to thumbing the ball. The index finger and middle finger "fork" the center of the ball and are the last fingers on the ball. If the hand is too much to the right side of the ball, for a right-handed shooter, it leads to two-handed shooting or unnecessary wrist rotation; if the middle finger is in the middle of the ball, it puts too much emphasis on the outside of the hand, and leads to an inside-out shooting motion.

Twisted Wrist

Some shooters start the shooting motion with the shooting hand on the ball's side – not behind the ball – like a two-handed set shot or the hand position for a volleyball set (left). As part of their technique, they turn their wrist to get their shooting hand under the ball, which is wasted motion that affects the shot's consistency and the consistency of the follow-through.

Most coaches obsess on the elbow. I watched a coach bring the ball to his shooting position, with his elbow tucked in and his pinky finger on his shooting hand toward the rim. As he shot, his whole hand rotated so he finished with his index finger pointing to the rim.

Instead, point hand and wrist to the target at the set position, with wrist cocked. This adds consistency and eliminates any extra motion which affects the shot.

Elbow Askew

The more the elbow escapes alignment, the greater the shot's inconsistency, as it adds a variable for the player to control. If the elbow moves too far from alignment, it changes the hand position, forcing a rotation of the wrist during the shot; or, the follow-through occurs to the left-side of the body, as that is where the arm extends from a position with an angled elbow alignment.

Because this adds variables and inconsistency to the technique, learning to shoot with the elbow in alignment increases the shooter's success. A proper elbow alignment sets the rest of the body position and guides the proper technique.

Thumbing the Ball

The off-hand imparts only a contra-productive force. It is used to balance the ball and guide the ball to the release. Many players "thumb" the ball with their off-hand (right); the left thumb of a right-handed shooter pushes forward, and the hands end with both palms facing the target. This imparts a force that counters the alignment and works against the shooter. The hand should fall off the ball as the wrist begins its flexion; a perfect follow-through finishes with the side of the pinky finger of the off-hand toward the target.

Errant Follow-Through

Players using too much upper body force push their follow-through; a right-handed shooter ends with his arm toward the left side of his body, not in a straight line to the target (Picture 1). Another flaw is short-arming the ball like Shawn Marion; the elbow fails to reach full extension (picture 2). Finally, some players "snap back." As they release the ball, their hand and arm recoil.

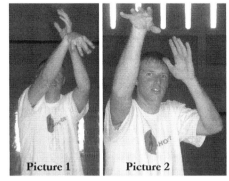

Picture 1   Picture 2

The follow-through must be straight to the target. If the body is aligned properly, a correct follow-through shoots the ball straight to the basket. If the follow-through is pushed to the left, the player should use more leg power. If short arming the ball, concentrate on reaching full extension, shooting the ball higher. If the player "snaps back," focus on being strong with the follow-through and holding it until the ball hits the net. Shooting Coach Dave Hopla tells players to "Freeze" their follow-through.

Hip Extension

Some players, especially girls, fail to extend at the hip; as they shoot, their legs extend and their upper body extends, but they stay flexed at the hip, with their butt out (picture to the right). This often leads to a slight backwards motion in their jump and counters the ball's movement. Like a person standing from a seated position, extend the hips so the shooter is erect; in shooting, the player should finish the shot in the same erect position, requiring the hips to extend (picture at left).

Appendix II:
Alignment and Shooting Biomechanics

Some players and coaches like only what is essential, while others want every detail. For those who are detail-oriented, I have enclosed the section on body alignment and shooting biomechanics from my original graduate school papers. While the text covers most of the concepts, this answers more detailed questions.

Alignment (Right-handed Shooter)

The "L" in BELIEF, alignment or "a line," is the body position attained through a proper shot preparation. Proper alignment provides the starting point for the technique.

Right Foot	Pointed at the target. Weight evenly distributed between each foot. Right foot slightly forward in a heel-toe relationship with the left foot.
Right Elbow	Tight to the body. The upper arm and lower arm form a 90-degree angle at the elbow joint.
Right Wrist	Fully extended. Wrinkle in the wrist as the ball is "cocked." The wrist is cocked in the shot pocket before any upward shooting motion.
Right Hand	Palm directed toward the basket with fingers to the sky.
Right-hand Fingers	Spread comfortably and applying pressure to the ball. The finger pads and calluses touch the ball; there is a slight gap between the ball and the palm of the hand.
Index Finger	In the middle of the ball. The index finger and the middle finger "fork" the center of the ball, while the index finger and the thumb form the shape of a "J."
Left Hand	Positioned on the side of the ball. The thumb of the right hand and the thumb of the left hand form an extended "T," though they should not touch or be too close together.

Shot Technique

Regardless of shot, the technique is the same; the shot preparation differs from shot to shot. However, once the ball is aligned in the shot pocket, the shot proceeds in the same manner every time with the power derived from the legs and the arm extending up and to the basket.

The shot starts with a forceful ankle, knee and hip extension, which provides sufficient force and vertical velocity. The vertical velocity is important, as the greater the arc, the greater the landing surface. A lower angle of release and lower height of release reduces the available surface area.

From the shot pocket (Hard2Guard position), the shoulder rotates upward, raising the elbow. The elbow rises to between shoulder height and eye level, depending on the shooter's strength. A shooter needing more strength or shooting further from the basket starts his elbow extension earlier and lower to the ground than a stronger shooter or one shooting closer to the basket. The degree of shoulder rotation affects the height and angle of release. A higher release and a greater angle of release create a higher shot. Many shooters miss because their shots are flat and have little room between the bottom of the ball and the rim, even at the shot's apex. A 52-55-degree angle of release is optimal, but the height of release impacts the release angle (Hay). A shorter shooter must shoot with a greater angle than a taller shooter. A taller shooter should not shoot flat; as all shooters aim for a 55-degree angle of release. For a visual, I tell players that when shooting a free throw, the ball should be above the top of the backboard at the shot's apex.

As the elbow nears the desired height (between shoulder and eye level), the elbow extends. As the elbow extends, the shoulder continues to rotate. The hand pushes up and through the ball.

The off-hand remains on the ball as the elbow extends. As the elbow nears full extension, the wrist flexion occurs. As the shooting hand moves forward, the off-hand falls off the ball. In this way, the off-hand does not impart a force on the ball; it provides balance and support until the release. As Dave Hopla says, the "off-hand" is the "miss-guide" hand as its only affect is negative.

As the wrist flexes, the fingers remain spread. Finish with knees fully extended, elbow fully extended and index finger pointing at the front of the rim. The shot's release occurs before the top of the jump; the further the shot, the earlier the player releases the ball.

Mechanics	Explanation
Ankle/Knee Extension	The ankle extension starts the shot. During the shot preparation, the ankles and knees flex to absorb the force of the ground impact. The body applies a force on the ground to create an upward force to propel the ball with a vertical velocity toward the basket.
Hip Extension	The hip extends so the trunk is nearly vertical as the shooter releases the ball.
Shoulder Rotation	As the lower body extends, the shoulder rotates upward, elevating the elbow.
Elbow Extension	The elbow lifts the ball to its release point.
Wrist Flexion	As the elbow nears complete extension, the wrist flexes. The hand pushes up and through the ball.
Eyes	The eyes fine center on the target and remain fixed on the target to keep the head still.
Alignment	Often the deceleration is incomplete in the shot preparation and the body drifts or rotates. The body should remain still throughout the shot.
Finish	Land on balance, slightly ahead of your take-off spot. Relax your hand with your fingers wide and your index finger pointed at the rim.

Q&A

Where do I start with a varsity player?

Without seeing the player, it is difficult to assess his starting position. If he is not an accurate, consistent shooter, start in Phase 1 and progress through all the steps, re-learning the correct technique. If he is a good shooter, and his form looks good (scores a 5 on the Phase 1 Matrix), focus on the first three phases and incorporate some aspects of the fourth phase. I do not progress to the fifth phase unless the player is absolutely perfect in the first four stages. If there is any question on the consistency of his technique, balance, footwork, or any other aspect, we fix the issue and improve his technique before graduating to the fifth phase.

For a player struggling with his shot, he may need to unlearn his technique and relearn a better technique. To guide a player through the process, diagnose his major flaws. After several shots, tell the player his biggest mistakes. Then, demonstrate proper shooting technique, addressing the major flaws. After demonstrating the new corrected mechanics, demonstrate his old method and explain the differences. Have the player mimic his old shot and the new method and ask him to explain and demonstrate the difference. Once he understands and illustrates the difference, he has the awareness to erase the old method and build the new way. From this point, practice the new way with regular feedback.

When do I move from one phase to the next?

I hate to answer a question with a question, but, "How good do you want to be?" I think it is John Wooden who said, "If you don't have time to do it properly now, when will you have time to re-do it?" Dave Hopla addressed his shooting camp by saying, "Good is the enemy of great." In general, that answers the question. Specifically, I train a mid-Division I recruit who spends 80% of his workout in the first three stages.

I think you progress to the next phase when your shooting is excellent. What is excellent? The book's objective is to develop a 180 Shooter; a player whose free throw percentage, field goal percentage and three-point percentage total 180. In a game, percentages suffer from defense, fatigue and pressure and are lower than shooting without defense. We aim for 75% in drills. In form shooting drills, varsity players make 15 shots in a row before we move to the next drill; no exceptions. Younger players make 12 in a row and beginners make nine in a row. If a player is not shooting 75% or better during drills, we do not shoot three-pointers in the workout.

I worked with a college player one summer to change her shooting mechanics so she could shoot off the dribble and shoot quicker off cuts. She had summer league games and in previous years, her role was as a stand-still three-point shooter. I asked her not to shoot any threes in her games; she was just starting the progression and I did not want her focused on the results. She listened, and by summer' end, she was shooting three-pointers with consistency and a new, improved shooting technique. She had the discipline to improve. She did not allow her good shooting to interfere with her desire to be a great shooter.

How many shots do I need to shoot?

Again, how good do you want to be? Experts believe it takes about 10,000 repetitions to develop a skill. NBA players typically take between 500-1000 shots a day in the off-season. The players I train shoot about 300 shots in a one-hour workout.

More important than the volume is the quality. In my workouts, we only count makes. According to psychologist K Anders Ericsson, concentrated effort in the direction of a desired goal is necessary to improve once a player has reached a base level of proficiency. He calls this deliberate practice, and it requires immediate and accurate feedback.

Practice alone is insufficient; deliberate practice is necessary. You can maintain the concentration required for deliberate practice for only a short amount of time (about an hour depending on maturity and fitness), which limits the quantity. However, to be a great shooter, a player should engage in some form of deliberate practice daily.

How much shooting should we do during the season?

I disagree with those coaches who do not believe a player can improve his or her shooting during the season. When I coach teams, we work diligently on shooting every day. I do not believe there is a more important skill in basketball. It depends on your system and the shooters on your team, but shooting accounts for 15-20% of my practice time during the season. Make small improvements day by day and by season's end you will see a big improvement.

How do I use the drills and phases with my team?

Team practices are difficult because a coach has so much to do to prepare his team. However, a good coach learns to prioritize. I use some team shooting drills, but I prefer to use all the baskets and get as many players shooting at a time as possible. I hate lines. Most team drills I use depend on our offense. I design shooting drills around the offensive system and use the drills to teach general shooting fundamentals and reinforce the system. As an example I used with a professional team, check out <u>Blitz Basketball</u>. Another method to use the progressions during practice is to use Phase 1 as a shooting warm-up every practice; cycle through the different phases each day, so Monday focuses on movement, Tuesday on shooting off the dribble, and Wednesday on game shots based on your system. Each week is a mini-progression, so each player practices the general shots and has an opportunity to improve his shooting technique and confidence. Finally, a coach can create shooting groups based on the progressions and place players into groups according to their current skill level. The groups dictate each player's shooting practice and set guidelines for his game shooting range. The groupings motivate players to practice in order to graduate to the next level and expand their freedom within the offense.

How do I give feedback when there are 12 players and one coach?

The large player to coach ratio hinders ideal teaching. Encourage player to player teaching. To facilitate this, the coach must create a positive learning environment and good team chemistry so each player understands that his partner is helping him improve his skill, not criticizing him. The coach can draw each partner's attention to each player's major flaws or limitations. If a player tends to receive a pass off-balance, the partner focuses on balance and instructs accordingly.

Another option is to create drills where players shoot on one basket, enabling the coach to watch everyone. Prevent players from standing around too much. Be creative with the drill; players shoot at one end, receive feedback from the coach and then dribble to the other end for another shot, which eliminates some of the standing around. Another method is using video before practice to focus each player on his weaknesses or flaws.

How do you convince a player to change his technique?

John Wooden said, "Failure is never fatal, but failure to change might be." Changing a player's shot depends on age and experience. Most college coaches will not tinker with a player's shot because to unlearn his technique and relearn the proper technique may take a full season, so they live with the results because their job is to win games. At the high school level, it depends on the player's goals. If a player is unwilling to put in the time and effort, there is no sense tinkering and sabotaging his confidence.

The easiest way to get a player to change his shooting technique is to use my old mantra: "Practice in proportion to your aspirations." If the player aspires to play college basketball, but he has flaws in his shooting technique, relearning his technique may increase his opportunities at the next level. He must possess a good work ethic and the desire to improve, if he wants to play in college. Using the goal of playing in college works because the coach is helping the player to reach the player's goal (college ball) rather than just the coach's goal (improved shooting).

Sometimes this is not enough. I worked with a girl who was a high school senior when we started training together and she professed to have no desire to play in college. However, when her season ended, she committed to a DIII school. When we started, I asked about changing her shot; she was a good spot-up shooter, but she needed a lot of space and could not shoot off-the dribble or on the move. At the time, she said she was okay with her technique and her role as a spot-up shooter, even though she played point guard, and she just wanted to have a good senior season.

After a freshman season mired on the bench, she acquiesced and approached me about changing her shot. We spent the summer working on her technique and she returned to school a more versatile shooter. But, it only happened because she acknowledged the need and put in the effort to make change happen.

Every player wants to improve. Nobody wants to stay the same. Nobody actively chooses to be a bad player. However, not everyone is willing to make the effort to improve. There is a huge difference. At the high school level, the unlearning and relearning process is valuable for those willing to make the effort.

At the youth level, around junior high school when players have the strength to shoot properly, it is always a good idea to change a player's form. Many players peak early because they have good results because of their size or quickness advantage, but they plateau. Good is the enemy of great. While it may be a struggle, these players have 5+ years of competitive basketball ahead and their shooting ability may impact the length of their career. At this age, players likely have not moved into the Autonomous Stage, so relearning the proper technique is easier than with older shooters whose technique, if not results, is automatic.

Some players, often due to immaturity or self-consciousness, will resist the suggestion that change is needed. These players often have a Fixed Mindset and believe you are either born with the skill or not. Suggesting a need for improvement is an indictment of their ability, not an attempt to help them maximize their talent.

In these cases, work on their minds first. Shift their mindset to a Growth Mindset. I use stories of players I trained and the improvement they made through hard work, or I find an example of an NBA player and use an article or story about the player and their growth (Kevin Durant, Kobe Bryant and others). However, our natural inclination is to assume NBA players are superhuman; therefore, I like to use stories of average kids from similar neighborhoods who made a great transformation when they changed their shooting form. I often use Matt Glynn, mentioned in Phase 1, as an example because he is an average looking kid who was an average high school player who decided he did not want to be average.

How do you teach shot selection?

Shot selection returns to the discussion of a player's range and his scoring zone from Phase 4. Dick DeVenzio, in one of his books, discusses shot selection and rates shots from a 1-9. But, what is and is not a good shot? Also, how do you tell a player not to shoot without ruining his confidence by telling him not to shoot?

When I coached a team that went to AAU Nationals, we had a couple players who shot threes. They were too young and probably should not have been shooting threes, but I was a young coach and we were a small team who could not rely on shooting lay-ups on every possession; at least a missed shot produced a chance for an offensive rebound against a zone defense.

After one game when a non-shooter took a three-pointer, another non-shooter asked if he could shoot threes. I asked if he thought he could make 50%. He said no. I asked if he thought he should shoot a shot if he cannot make 50%. He said probably not. Problem solved.

I hate to tell players not to shoot. My freshman high school coach made a team full of shooters a terrible shooting team because he second-guessed every miss and instituted a five-pass rule. We never knew if we were allowed to shoot or not. I remember in one game I hit a couple shots early, and a friend on the other team started talking trash to me, and I completely forgot my coach and our rules and just played; it was my best game and the individual season high for our team. Otherwise, our coach's restrictions hampered our confidence.

I believe good shooters are confident shooters and I do not believe any player shoots with confidence if he wonders if his coach is going to yank him out of the game if he misses. I know a current NCAA Division I player who never looked comfortable playing or shooting with his high school team because his coach is notorious for yanking players out of the game for any small mistake or missed shot. This fear of failure is often stronger than an individual's personal confidence. Therefore, shot selection is difficult for me as a coach because I believe so strongly in the power of confidence and self-fulfilling prophecies.

NBA and WNBA coach Paul Westhead said about shot selection when talking about Kevin Durant's low shooting percentages during his rookie season:

> "You're asking the wrong guy—and the reason I say that is, my players, from good teams or bad teams, will say to you that I never saw a bad shot by a player on my team. They can't take a bad shot.
>
> I want to give them the freedom to create what they think are good shots and once you start stipulating that I want you to shoot from here but not there and I want you to shoot this but not that then you start putting things in their minds that they have to make hard decisions about at a moment when they should be focusing on the basket.
>
> If you let a player take 15 or 20 shots, he might take what the world might say are a couple bad shots but he doesn't want to take bad shots. He's not going to go from three bad shots to eight bad shots because you don't say anything to him. He'll eliminate those bad shots–or at least cut down on them–on his own," (Friedman).

I encourage any player to shoot a good shot. A good shot, however, varies from individual to individual, but it is an open shot within a player's scoring zone. The player's view of his scoring zone and the coach's view may differ. However, as a coach, I do not take players out of the game for taking a bad shot and I do not criticize it during the game. It is a teaching point for practice. To determine the player's scoring zone, he must hit consistently from a spot during practice. Consistently is another vague term, and it differs by age group. An eight-year-old novice may not make lay-ups consistently, let alone jump shots, but he or she still has to be encouraged to shoot during a game, or he or she will never enjoy the experience. A varsity player, on the other hand, should hit 70+% of his practice shots for the spot to be inside his scoring zone.

What makes a great shooting coach?

A coach must know his stuff and be a good communicator: one without the other is insufficient. A mathematical genius knows his stuff, but if he is not a good communicator, he will not be a successful teacher because teaching requires performance or learning from someone else (student/player). Sometimes the curse of knowledge interferes and an expert is unable to teach a less experienced player because he cannot remember what it is like not to be an expert. A shooting coach must know shooting, but he also must relate to the player to improve his communication.

When coaching a team, motivation, leadership skills, player evaluation and more determine a coach's success (not to mention the talent). However, while these skills impact an individual trainer or shooting coach, they are secondary.

When I watch other trainers, the good trainers run organized, logical workouts which have a natural flow or progression. A trainer is not a good trainer because he runs an organized, logical, progressive workout; this is a starting point. I do not believe following step-back jump shots with form shooting is logical. The five phases describe a general learning procession and my teaching progression, and illustrate the general order I use in an individual workout. If a player has moved into the fourth phase, we start with form shooting and use general drills from Phase 2 and 3 as a warm-up before engaging in new shots or more game specific shots. That is not the only way to organize a workout, but it is logical and progressive.

The problem with many coaches is that workouts are marketing propaganda and trainers/coaches believe parents want to see kids doing advanced drills before they hire the trainer/coach. Trainers eschew basic shots and form shooting because it is not advanced and does not sell. I watched a trainer do step-back jump shots with a nine-year-old who could not make a lay-up. The kid probably made ten shots in an hour. But, when his dad arrived, the kid boasted, "I learned Bobby Jackson's step-back, daddy," as he demonstrated the move and threw the ball off the top of the backboard. The dad thought it was great. Maybe the enthusiasm from learning an NBA player's move is worth it, but the player actually got worse in the hour.

I trained a 10-year-old whose father was a very successful high school coach. We never shot past the elbow because that is where his form broke down, but he made about 75% of his shots, as he made 12 shots in a row in our stationary shooting drills. The father was pleased with the workouts and his son's progress. During one workout, the father told me that a mother of a girl working out at the facility watched the workout and said it was too simple. She bragged that her seven-year-old did more advanced things with her trainer. This is a problem for trainers; every workout is marketing and parents cannot differentiate the good from bad, but they can differentiate hard and advanced. In this situation, the mom was about 5'3, so the chances she played basketball at a high level are small, while the father coached one of the area's best high school teams and developed an NBA player.

A good shooting coach should be able to diagnose the problem and devise a program to improve the limitation, and gradually, but consistently elevate the player's performance. An organized, progressive workout is important, but the coach also needs the flexibility to change paths if a new problem arises. I view shooting instruction as problem solving, which is what I enjoy. But beyond the diagnosis and the program, he must be able to reach and relate to the player and to meet his individual learning needs.

Individual Drills

Phase 1

Wooden's Jump Shot Drill: Stand in front of the basket in an athletic position without a ball. Shoot a jump shot. Land, prepare to shoot and repeat. Shoot 25. Visualize making each shot. *Form Shooting*

Three in a row Shooting Drill: Start directly in front of the basket. Use proper form and shoot. Make three shots in a row to take a step back. Start over at the beginning on a miss. Youth players make nine shots in a row; varsity high school players make 15 shots in a row. *Form Shooting; Section 2 and 6*

Three Swishes Drill: Start directly in front of the basket. Use proper form and shoot. Swish three in a row to take a step back. If you make a basket, but not a swish, remain at the current spot. On a miss, take one step forward. Work to the free throw line. *Form Shooting; Section 2 and 6*

Nowitski Shooting Drill: Start in the middle of the key with the ball at the set position. Bend into a full squat, extend and shoot. Make 10. *Form Shooting; Section 6*

3x5 Shooting Drill: Start in the middle of the lane. Start with one leg forward and step-in to each shot. Make five in a row with the right leg forward and five in a row with the left leg forward. Move back and repeat. Shoot from three spots. *Form Shooting; Section 2 and 6*

15 Shooting Drill: Start in the middle of the lane and make five straight jump shots. After five straight, take a step back. Make 15 straight shots: all jump shots with complete lift and extension. Start over on a miss. Shoot for 2:00. *Catch-and-Shoot; Section 2 and 6*

Slide Shooting Drill: Start at one elbow and shuffle to the other elbow. Catch and shoot. Finish the release, get back into an athletic stance and shuffle to the other elbow for a shot. Make 10. *Catch-and-Shoot; Section 6*

Arc Slide Shooting Drill: Start on the baseline about 15-feet from the basket in an athletic position ready to catch and shoot. Shuffle around the perimeter. Catch and shoot. Finish the release, get back into an athletic stance and continue shuffling. Work from baseline to baseline and back. *Catch-and-Shoot; Section 4, 5, 6, 7 and 8*

5x5 Shooting Drill: Shoot mid-range jump shots from each baseline, each wing and the middle; make five shots at each spot and then move to the next spot. Make 25 shots total. *Catch-and-Shoot; Section 4, 5, 6, 7 and 8*

3-Point Arc Slide Shooting Drill: Start on the baseline at the three-point line in an athletic position ready to catch and shoot. Shuffle around the perimeter. Catch and shoot. Finish the release, get back into an athletic stance and continue shuffling. Work from baseline to baseline and back. *Catch-and-Shoot; Section 9, 10, 11, 12, 13, 14 and 15*

3-Point 5x5 Shooting Drill: Shoot mid-range jump shots from each baseline, each wing and the middle; make five shots at each spot and then move to the next spot. Make 25 shots total. *Catch-and-Shoot; Section 9, 10, 11, 12, 13, 14 and 15*

Phase 2

Straight-line Shooting: Start between half-court and the free throw line, run to the free throw line, catch and shoot. Use a left-right 1-2-step for one set and a right-left 1-2-step for the next set. Make five shots to start and progress accordingly. If working in pairs, alternate shots: shoot, rebound and pass to your partner before returning to the starting point. *Catch-and-Shoot; Section 6*

3-Point Straight-line Shooting: Start at half-court, run to the top of the key, catch and shoot. Use a left-right 1-2-step for one set and a right-left 1-2-step for the next set. Also, use the wings and the baseline, but run straight at the basket with feet, hips and shoulders squared. If working in pairs, alternate shots: shoot, rebound and pass to your partner before returning to the starting point. *Catch-and-Shoot; Section 12*

Right Wing Straight-line Shooting: Start at the hash mark on the right sideline, run to the basket, catch about 15-feet from the basket and shoot. Step in left-right. Make five shots to start and progress accordingly. If working in pairs, alternate shots: shoot, rebound and pass to your partner before returning to the starting point. *Catch-and-Shoot; Section 5*

Left Wing Straight-line Shooting: Start at the hash mark on the left sideline, run to the basket, catch about 15-feet from the basket and shoot. Step in right-left. Make five shots to start and progress accordingly. If working in pairs, alternate shots: shoot, rebound and pass to your partner before returning to the starting point. *Catch-and-Shoot; Section 7*

Right Wing 3-Point Straight-line Shooting: Start at the hash mark on the right sideline, run to the basket, catch at the three-point line and shoot. Step-in left-right. Make five shots to start and progress accordingly. If working in pairs, alternate shots: shoot, rebound and pass to your partner before returning to the starting point. *Catch-and-Shoot; Section 10*

Left Wing 3-Point Straight-line Shooting: Start at the hash mark on the left sideline, run to the basket, catch at the three-point line and shoot. Step in right-left. Make five shots to start and progress accordingly. If working in pairs, alternate shots: shoot, rebound and pass to your partner before returning to the starting point. *Catch-and-Shoot; Section 14*

Elbow-to-Elbow Shooting Drill: Start at one elbow and run to the other elbow by tracing the half-circle above the free throw line. Catch with an inside foot 1-2-step and shoot. Make six to start and progress accordingly. *Catch-and-Shoot; Curl; Section 6*

Right Corner Curls Shooting Drill: Start in the right corner and curl to the right elbow, catch and shoot. Jog to the corner and repeat. Make five. *Catch-and-Shoot; Curl; Section 6*

Left Corner Curls Shooting Drill: Start in the left corner and curl to the left elbow, catch and shoot. Jog to the corner and repeat. Make five. *Catch-and-Shoot; Curl; Section 6*

3-Point Right Corner Curls Shooting Drill: Start in the right corner and curl to the three-point line above the elbow, catch and shoot. Jog to the corner and repeat. Make five. *Catch-and-Shoot; Curl; Section 11*

3-Point Left Corner Curls Shooting Drill: Start in the left corner and curl to the three-point line above the elbow, catch and shoot. Jog to the corner and repeat. Make five. *Catch-and-Shoot; Curl; Section 13*

Five-Spot Shooting Drill: Shoot mid-range jump shots from each baseline, each wing and the middle; make one shot and move to the next spot. After the first shot, shoot two in a row in the corners. Make 25. *Catch-and-Shoot; Section 4, 5, 6, 7 and 8*

3-point Five-Spot Shooting Drill: Shoot three-point jump shots from each baseline, each wing and the middle; make one shot and move to the next spot. After the first shot, shoot two in a row in the corners. Make 25. *Catch-and-Shoot; Section 9, 10, 12, 14 and 15*

Homer's Seven Spot Series Shooting Drill: Place seven chairs around the perimeter in the player's shooting range, roughly on the baselines, the 45-degree angles, the elbows and the top of the key. Start under the basket and pass the ball to a partner/coach. Curl around the first chair, catch, shoot, rebound, pass to the coach again and move to the next chair. Work through all seven chairs and then back to the starting point. On the second time through, pump fake, explode to the basket and finish with a lay-up. Work once through the seven chairs with a left-handed dribble and once with a right-handed dribble. *Catch-and-Shoot; Section 4, 5, 6, 7 and 8*

Olympic Shooting Drill: Player 1 shoots until he misses and Player 2 rebounds. Shots in the paint are worth 1 point; 10-foot bank shots are 2 points; free throw line jumpers are 2 points; three-pointers are three points. Shooter must keep moving and catch in shooting position with knees bent. Teams shoot for 2:00. **Tag**: *Catch-and-Shoot; Section 6 (1-point shots), Section 5, 6 and 7 (2-point shots), Section 9, 10, 11, 12, 13, 14 and 15 (3-point shots)*

Phase 3

Two-Dribble Pull-ups Shooting Drill (right hand): Start beyond the three-point line and use two dribbles to get to a mid-range jump shot at the free throw line. Use right hand dribble. Stop on-balance and shoot. Rebound your shot. *Off-the-Dribble; Section 6*

Two-Dribble Pull-ups Shooting Drill (left hand): Start beyond the three-point line and use two dribbles to get to a mid-range jump shot at the free throw line. Use left hand dribble. Stop on-balance and shoot. Rebound your shot. *Off-the-Dribble; Section 6*

3-Point Two-Dribble Pull-ups Shooting Drill (right hand): Start near half-court and use two dribbles to get to the three-point line. Use right hand dribble. Stop on-balance and shoot. Rebound your shot. *Off-the-Dribble; Section 12*

3-Point Two-Dribble Pull-ups Shooting Drill (left hand): Start near half-court and use two dribbles to get to the three-point line. Use left hand dribble. Stop on-balance and shoot. Rebound your shot. *Off-the-Dribble; Section 12*

Right Wing Two-Dribble Pull-ups Shooting Drill (right hand): Start beyond the three-point line and use two dribbles to get to a mid-range jump shot on the right wing. Dribble with the right hand. Rebound your shot. *Off-the-Dribble; Section 5*

Left Wing Two-Dribble Pull-ups Shooting Drill (left hand): Start beyond the three-point line and use two dribbles to get to a mid-range jump shot on the left wing. Dribble with the left hand. Rebound your shot. *Off-the-Dribble; Section 7*

Right Elbow Two-Dribble Pull-ups Shooting Drill (left hand): Start beyond the three-point line on the right wing and use two dribbles to get to a mid-range jump shot at the elbow. Dribble with the left hand. Rebound your shot. *Off-the-Dribble; Section 6*

Left Elbow Two-Dribble Pull-ups Shooting Drill (right hand): Start beyond the three-point line on the left wing and use two dribbles to get to a mid-range jump shot at the elbow. Dribble with the right hand. Rebound your shot. *Off-the-Dribble; Section 6*

3-Point Wing Two-Dribble Pull-ups Shooting Drill (right hand): Start beyond the three-point line and use two dribbles to get to a three-point jump shot on the right wing. Dribble with the right hand. Stop on-balance and shoot. Rebound your shot. *Off-the-Dribble; Section 10*

3-Point Wing Two-Dribble Pull-ups Shooting Drill (left hand): Start beyond the three-point line and use two dribbles to get to a three-point jump shot on the left wing. Dribble with the left hand. Stop on-balance and shoot. Rebound your shot. *Off-the-Dribble; Section 14*

Inside Hand Two-Dribble Pull-ups Shooting Drill (left hand): Start on the right side near half-court and attack toward the elbow with the inside hand. Use two dribbles to get to a three-point jump shot on the right side. Dribble with the left hand. Stop on-balance and shoot. Rebound your shot. *Off-the-Dribble; Section 11*

Inside Hand Two-Dribble Pull-ups Shooting Drill (right hand): Start on the left side near half-court and attack toward the elbow with the inside hand. Use two dribbles to get to a three-point jump shot on the left side. Dribble with the right hand. Stop on-balance and shoot. Rebound your shot. *Off-the-Dribble; Section 13*

Side Pick-and-Roll Pull-up Jump Shot Series

- **Right Side Pick-and-Roll Pull-up Jump Shot Series:** Start on the right side of the court near half court. Dribble the ball down to the three-point line and make a change of direction move (protect spin, pull-back crossover, behind-the-back). Imagine a teammate setting an on-ball screen or use a cone. Hesitate and then penetrate with the left hand toward the middle of the court. Use two dribbles to curl into a pull-up jump shot at the elbow. *Off-the-Dribble; Section 6*
- **Left Side Pick-and-Roll Pull-up Jump Shot Series:** Start on the left side of the court near half court. Dribble the ball down to the three-point line and make a change of direction move (protect spin, pull-back crossover, behind-the-back). Imagine a teammate setting an on-ball screen or use a cone. Hesitate and then penetrate with the right hand toward the middle of the court. Use two dribbles to curl into a pull-up jump shot at the elbow. *Off-the-Dribble; Section 6*

Mike Bibby Pull-up Jump Shot Series

- **Right Side Bibby over-the-Top:** Start on the right side of the court near half court. Speed dribble with the left hand; as you near the three-point line, switch to a protect dribble and shuffle forward with the ball in the left hand and body open to the middle of the court. Around the free throw line extended, hesitate with a quick in-n-out dribble and penetrate with the left hand to the middle of the floor. Stop and shoot. **Tag**: *Off-the-Dribble; Section 6*
- **Right Side Bibby Crossover:** Start on the right side of the court near half court. Speed dribble with the left hand; as you near the three-point line, switch to a protect dribble and shuffle forward with the ball in the left hand and body open to the middle of the court. Around the free throw line extended, hesitate and crossover. Attack with the right hand, stop and shoot. *Off-the-Dribble; Section 5*
- **Left Side Bibby over-the-Top:** Start on the left side of the court near half court. Speed dribble with the right hand; as you near the three-point line, switch to a protect dribble and shuffle forward with the ball in the right hand and body open to the middle of the court. Around the free throw line extended, hesitate with a quick in-n-out dribble and penetrate with the right hand to the middle of the floor. Stop and shoot. *Off-the-Dribble; Section 6*

- **Left Side Bibby Crossover:** Start on the left side of the court near half court. Speed dribble with the right hand; as you near the three-point line, switch to a protect dribble and shuffle forward with the ball in the right hand and body open to the middle of the court. Around the free throw line extended, hesitate and crossover. Attack with the left hand, stop and shoot. *Off-the-Dribble; Section 7*

Full Court Pull-ups Shooting Drill: Dribble the length of the floor and pull-up for jump shots at various angles within the shooter's range. Vary each shot, adding hesitations, fakes, step-backs, etc to make the shots more game-like. Dribble with both hands. *Off-the-dribble, Section 6, 7 and 8*

Direct Drive One-Dribble Pull-ups (left pivot): Start at the top of the key; shot fake, take one dribble toward the basket and shoot. Use the left foot as the pivot foot; make a direct drive and dribble with the right hand. *Off-the-dribble; Section 6*

Crossover Drive One-Dribble Pull-ups (left pivot): Start at the top of the key; shot fake, take one dribble toward the basket and shoot. Use the left foot as the pivot foot; make a crossover drive and dribble with the left hand. *Off-the-dribble; Section 6*

Direct Drive One-Dribble Pull-ups (right pivot): Start at the top of the key; shot fake, take one dribble toward the basket and shoot. Use the right foot as the pivot foot; make a direct drive and dribble with the left hand. *Off-the-dribble; Section 6*

Crossover Drive One-Dribble Pull-ups (right pivot): Start at the top of the key; shot fake, take one dribble toward the basket and shoot. Use the right foot as the pivot foot; make a crossover drive and dribble with the right hand. *Off-the-dribble; Section 6*

Right Wing Direct Drive One-Dribble Pull-ups (left pivot): Start on the right wing at a 45-degree angle; shot fake, take one dribble toward the basket and shoot. Use the left foot as the pivot foot; make a direct drive and dribble with the right hand. *Off-the-dribble; Section 5*

Right Wing Crossover Drive One-Dribble Pull-ups (left pivot): Start on the right wing at a 45-degree angle; shot fake, take one dribble toward the basket and shoot. Use the left foot as the pivot foot; make a crossover drive and dribble with the left hand. *Off-the-dribble; Section 5*

Right Wing Direct Drive One-Dribble Pull-ups (right pivot): Start on the right wing at a 45-degree angle; shot fake, take one dribble toward the basket and shoot. Use the right foot as the pivot foot; make a direct drive and dribble with the left hand. *Off-the-dribble; Section 5*

Right Wing Crossover Drive One-Dribble Pull-ups (right pivot): Start on the right wing at a 45-degree angle; shot fake, take one dribble toward the basket and shoot. Use the right foot as the pivot foot; make a crossover drive and dribble with the right hand. *Off-the-dribble; Section 5*

Left Wing Direct Drive One-Dribble Pull-ups (left pivot): Start on the left wing at a 45-degree angle; shot fake, take one dribble toward the basket and shoot. Use the left foot as the pivot foot; make a direct drive and dribble with the right hand. *Off-the-dribble; Section 7*

Left Wing Crossover Drive One-Dribble Pull-ups (left pivot): Start on the left wing at a 45-degree angle; shot fake, take one dribble toward the basket and shoot. Use the left foot as the pivot foot; make a crossover drive and dribble with the left hand. *Off-the-dribble; Section 7*

Left Wing Direct Drive One-Dribble Pull-ups (right pivot): Start on the left wing at a 45-degree angle; shot fake, take one dribble toward the basket and shoot. Use the right foot as the pivot foot; make a direct drive and dribble with the left hand. *Off-the-dribble; Section 7*

Left Wing Crossover Drive One-Dribble Pull-ups (right pivot): Start on the left wing at a 45-degree angle; shot fake, take one dribble toward the basket and shoot. Use the right foot as the pivot foot; make a crossover drive and dribble with the right hand. *Off-the-dribble; Section 7*

Right Corner Direct Drive One-Dribble Pull-ups (left pivot): Start in the right corner; shot fake, take one dribble toward the basket and shoot. Use the left foot as the pivot foot; make a direct drive and dribble with the right hand. *Off-the-dribble; Section 4*

Right Corner Crossover Drive One-Dribble Pull-ups (left pivot): Start in the right corner; shot fake, take one dribble toward the basket and shoot. Use the left foot as the pivot foot; make a crossover drive and dribble with the left hand. *Off-the-dribble; Section 4*

Right Corner Direct Drive One-Dribble Pull-ups (right pivot): Start in the right corner; shot fake, take one dribble toward the basket and shoot. Use the right foot as the pivot foot; make a direct drive and dribble with the left hand. *Off-the-dribble; Section 4*

Right Corner Crossover Drive One-Dribble Pull-ups (right pivot): Start in the right corner; shot fake, take one dribble toward the basket and shoot. Use the right foot as the pivot foot; make a crossover drive and dribble with the right hand. *Off-the-dribble; Section 4*

Left Corner Direct Drive One-Dribble Pull-ups (left pivot): Start in the left corner; shot fake, take one dribble toward the basket and shoot. Use the left foot as the pivot foot; make a direct drive and dribble with the right hand. *Off-the-dribble; Section 8*

Left Corner Crossover Drive One-Dribble Pull-ups (left pivot): Start in the left corner; shot fake, take one dribble toward the basket and shoot. Use the left foot as the pivot foot; make a crossover drive and dribble with the left hand. *Off-the-dribble; Section 8*

Left Corner Direct Drive One-Dribble Pull-ups (right pivot): Start in the left corner; shot fake, take one dribble toward the basket and shoot. Use the right foot as the pivot foot; make a direct drive and dribble with the left hand. *Off-the-dribble; Section 8*

Left Corner Crossover Drive One-Dribble Pull-ups (right pivot): Start in the left corner; shot fake, take one dribble toward the basket and shoot. Use the right foot as the pivot foot; make a crossover drive and dribble with the right hand. *Off-the-dribble; Section 8*

Arc Slide Right Hand One-Dribble Pull-ups: Start in the right baseline corner at the three-point line in an athletic position ready to catch and shoot. Shuffle around the perimeter. Catch, take one dribble with the right hand and shoot. Finish the release, return to the three-point line, get into an athletic stance and continue shuffling. Work from baseline to baseline. *Off-the-Dribble, Section 4, 5, 6, 7 and 8*

Arc Slide Left Hand One-Dribble Pull-ups: Start in the right baseline corner at the three-point line in an athletic position ready to catch and shoot. Shuffle around the perimeter. Catch, take one dribble with the left hand and shoot. Finish the release, return to the three-point line, get into an athletic stance and continue shuffling. Work from baseline to baseline. *Off-the-Dribble, Section 4, 5, 6, 7 and 8*

30 Shooting Drill: Shoot from five spots on the floor with three shots in each series. The first shot in each series is worth three points, second shot is worth two points and third shot is worth one point. Use the baseline on each side of the floor, 45-degree angle on each side, and the top of the key. Start under the basket, sprint to the sideline, cut towards the basket, receive the pass at three-point line and shoot. Return to the sideline and then cut to the basket. Catch the pass, execute a shot fake, take one dribble and shoot a pull-up jump shot. Return to the sideline and then cut to the basket. Catch at the three-point line, execute a shot fake, take one dribble and make a lay-up. Move to the next spot. Continue through all five spots for a possible total of 30 points. *Competition Drill*

Pirates' Shooting Drill: One player shoots, one rebounds/passes. Three minutes on the clock. Shooter shoots five consecutive mid-range jumpers that are worth one point as teammate rebounds and passes. Shooter must catch the ball on the move: no standing. Rotate every five shots. After one minute, shoot mid-range pull-up jumpers off one dribble that are worth two points. During minute three, shoot 3-point shots that are worth three points. Shooter keeps own score and passer ensures they rotate after five shots. Players compete against teammates or against a pre-determined, achievable goal. *First minute: Catch-and-Shoot; Section 4, 5, 6, 7 and 8; Second minute: Off-the Dribble; Section 4, 5, 6, 7 and 8; and Third Minute: Catch-and-Shoot; Section 9, 10, 11, 12, 13, 14 and 15*

Middle Open Court Moves Shooting Drill: Start at half court and combine open court offensive moves with pull-up jump shots. Set-up a chair at the top of the key as a defensive player and attack the chair, make a change of direction move, extend with the next dribble and hit the pull-up jump shot. Use a hesitation dribble, hard crossover, in-'n-out, or through-the-legs as well as double moves like a hesitation crossover or an in-n-out crossover. *Off-the-Dribble; Section 6*

Right Wing Open Court Moves Shooting Drill: Start at half court and combine open court offensive moves with pull-up jump shots. Set-up a chair on the right wing outside the three-point line as a defensive player and attack the chair, make a change of direction move, extend with the next dribble and hit the pull-up jump shot. Use a hesitation dribble, hard crossover, in-'n-out, or through-the-legs as well as double moves like a hesitation crossover or an in-n-out crossover. *Off-the-Dribble; Section 5*

Left Wing Open Court Moves Shooting Drill: Start at half court and combine open court offensive moves with pull-up jump shots. Set-up a chair on the left wing outside the three-point line as a defensive player and attack the chair, make a change of direction move, extend with the next dribble and hit the pull-up jump shot. Use a hesitation dribble, hard crossover, in-'n-out, or through-the-legs as well as double moves like a hesitation crossover or an in-n-out crossover. *Off-the-Dribble; Section 7*

Sit-on-It Shooting Series

- **Right Side Sit-on-It Baseline Drive Shots**: Start on the right side and penetrate toward the baseline with the right hand. Stop quickly with a hockey stop, squaring to the basket on the stop and dribbling the ball behind-the-back. Use the behind-the-back dribble to protect the ball from the defense and the quick stop to create space to shoot. *Off-the-Dribble; Section 4*
- **Right Side Sit-on-It Elbow Shots**: Start on the right side and penetrate toward the elbow with the left hand. Stop quickly with a hockey stop, squaring to the basket on the stop and dribbling the ball behind-the-back. Use the behind-the-back dribble to protect the ball from the defense and the quick stop to create space to shoot. *Off-the-Dribble; Section 6*
- **Left Side Sit-on-It Baseline Drive Shots**: Start on the left side and penetrate toward the baseline with the left hand. Stop quickly with a hockey stop, squaring to the basket on the stop and dribbling the ball behind-the-back. Use the behind-the-back dribble to protect the ball from the defense and the quick stop to create space to shoot. *Off-the-Dribble; Section 8*
- **Left Side Sit-on-It Elbow Shots**: Start on the left side and penetrate toward the elbow with the right hand. Stop quickly with a hockey stop, squaring to the basket on the stop and dribbling the ball behind-the-back. Use the behind-the-back dribble to protect the ball from the defense and the quick stop to create space to shoot. *Off-the-Dribble; Section 6*

Logger Drill: Place 6-7 chairs throughout the court, from free throw line to free throw line. Make 6 free throw line pull-up jumpers to complete the drill. Dribble from end to end and make an open court move (hard crossover, hesitation, in-and-out, around-the-back or through-the-legs) at a minimum of three chairs. *Off-the-Dribble; Section 6*

"If You Can Dodge a Wrench" Series: Start beyond the top of the key with the dribble. Attack toward the three-point line; do three consecutive offensive moves (crossover, behind-the-back, through-the-legs, in-n-out, around-the-back, or spin) and shoot. *Off-the-Dribble; Section 6*

Phase 4

Corner Curl Series

- **Right Corner Curl:** Start in the right corner; curl to the elbow, catch and shoot. Jog to the corner and repeat. Make five. *Catch-and-Shoot; Section 6*
- **Right Corner Curl and Crossover Drive**: Start in the right corner; curl to the elbow, catch, use a crossover step and one dribble with the right hand and shoot. Make five. *Off-the-dribble; Section 5*
- **Right Corner Curl and Run-Through:** Start in the right corner; curl to the elbow, run through the catch, using one dribble with the left hand to separate, and shoot. *Off-the-dribble; Section 6*
- **Left Corner Curl:** Start in the left corner; curl to the elbow, catch and shoot. Jog to the corner and repeat. Make five. *Catch-and-Shoot; Section 6*
- **Left Corner Curl and Crossover Drive**: Start in the left corner; curl to the elbow, catch, use a crossover step and one dribble with the left hand and shoot. Make five. *Off-the-dribble; Section 7*
- **Left Corner Curl and Run-Through:** Start in the left corner; curl to the elbow, run through the catch, using one dribble with the right hand to separate, and shoot. *Off-the-dribble; Section 6*

3-point Corner Curl Series

- **3-point Right Corner Curl:** Start in the right corner; curl to the three-point line above the elbow, catch and shoot. Jog to the corner and repeat. Make five. *Catch-and-Shoot; Section 11*
- **3-point Right Corner Curl and Crossover Drive**: Start in the right corner; curl to the three-point line above the elbow, catch, use a crossover step and one dribble with the right hand and shoot. Make five. *Off-the-dribble; Section 5*
- **3-point Right Corner Curl and Run-Through:** Start in the right corner; curl to the three-point line above the elbow, run through the catch, using one dribble with the left hand to separate, and shoot. *Off-the-dribble; Section 6*
- **3-point Left Corner Curl:** Start in the left corner; curl to the three-point line above the elbow, catch and shoot. Jog to the corner and repeat. Make five. *Catch-and-Shoot; Section 13*
- **3-point Left Corner Curl and Crossover Drive**: Start in the left corner; curl to the three-point line above the elbow, catch, use a crossover step and one dribble with the left hand and shoot. Make five. *Off-the-dribble; Section 7*
- **3-point Left Corner Curl and Run-Through:** Start in the left corner; curl to the three-point line above the elbow, run through the catch, using one dribble with the right hand to separate, and shoot. *Off-the-dribble; Section 6*

Flex Shooting Series

- **Flex Right Elbow Shot**: Start at the right block. Imagine setting a screen for the flex cutter. Cut to the right elbow, catch and shoot. *Catch-and-Shoot; Section 6*
- **Flex Right Corner Fade**: Start at the right block. Imagine setting a screen for the flex cutter. Begin the cut to the right elbow, fade to the corner, catch the skip pass and shoot. *Catch-and-Shoot; Section 4*
- **Flex Left Elbow Shot**: Start at the left block. Imagine setting a screen for the flex cutter. Cut to the left elbow, catch and shoot. *Catch-and-Shoot; Section 6*
- **Flex Left Corner Fade**: Start at the left block. Imagine setting a screen for the flex cutter. Begin the cut to the left elbow, fade to the corner, catch the skip pass and shoot. *Catch-and-Shoot; Section 8*

Flex 3-Point Shooting Series

- **Flex Right Side 3-point Shot**: Start at the right block. Imagine setting a screen for the flex cutter. Cut to the three-point line beyond the right elbow, catch and shoot. *Catch-and-Shoot; Section 11*
- **Flex Right Corner 3-point Fade**: Start at the right block. Imagine setting a screen for the flex cutter. Begin the cut to the right elbow, fade to the corner, catch the skip pass and shoot. *Catch-and-Shoot; Section 9*
- **Flex Left Side 3-point Shot**: Start at the left block. Imagine setting a screen for the flex cutter. Cut to the three-point line beyond the left elbow, catch and shoot. *Catch-and-Shoot; Section 13*
- **Flex Left Corner Fade**: Start at the left block. Imagine setting a screen for the flex cutter. Begin the cut to the left elbow, fade to the corner, catch the skip pass and shoot. *Catch-and-Shoot; Section 15*

Right Wing America's Play Shooting Drill: Start on the right block. Turn and set a cross screen in the middle of the key. Sprint to the top of the key, catch the pass from the right wing and shoot. Repeat. Make four. *Catch-and-Shoot; Section 12*

Left Wing America's Play Shooting Drill: Start on the left block. Turn and set a cross screen in the middle of the key. Sprint to the top of the key, catch the pass from the left wing and shoot. Repeat. Make four. *Catch-and-Shoot; Section 12*

Right Side Single-Double Baseline Series

- **Right Side Single-Double Tight Curl**: Start in the middle of the key. Set up a defender to the left and cut toward the right block. Imagine using a down screen (or use a cone or chair as a screener), as in a common single-double screen situation. Curl tight off the screen toward the elbow, catch and shoot. Make six. *Catch-and-Shoot; Section 6*
- **Right Side Single-Double Loose Curl**: Start in the middle of the key. Set up a defender to the left and cut toward the right block. Imagine using a down screen (or use a cone or chair as a screener), as in a common single-double screen situation. Curl loose off the screen to the wing beyond the three-point line, catch and shoot. Make six. *Catch-and-Shoot; Section 10*
- **Right Side Single-Double Loose Curl and Crossover Drive**: Start in the middle of the key. Set up a defender to the left and cut toward the right block. Imagine using a down screen (or use a cone or chair as a screener), as in a common single-double screen situation.

Curl loose off the screen to the wing beyond the three-point line, catch and rip-through, take one dribble toward the baseline and shoot. Make six. *Off-the-Dribble; Section 4*

- **Right Side Single-Double Fade**: Start in the middle of the key. Set up a defender to the left and cut toward the right block. Imagine using a down screen (or use a cone or chair as a screener), as in a common single-double screen situation. Fade to the corner beyond the three-point line, catch and shoot. Make six. *Catch-and-Shoot; Section 9*
- **Left Side Single-Double Tight Curl**: Start in the middle of the key. Set up a defender to the right and cut toward the left block. Imagine using a down screen (or use a cone or chair as a screener), as in a common single-double screen situation. Curl tight off the screen toward the elbow, catch and shoot. Make six. *Catch-and-Shoot; Section 6*
- **Left Side Single-Double Loose Curl**: Start in the middle of the key. Set up a defender to the right and cut toward the left block. Imagine using a down screen (or use a cone or chair as a screener), as in a common single-double screen situation. Curl loose off the screen to the wing beyond the three-point line, catch and shoot. Make six. *Catch-and-Shoot; Section 14*
- **Left Side Single-Double Loose Curl and Crossover Drive**: Start in the middle of the key. Set up a defender to the right and cut toward the left block. Imagine using a down screen (or use a cone or chair as a screener), as in a common single-double screen situation. Curl loose off the screen to the wing beyond the three-point line, catch and rip-through, take one dribble toward the baseline and shoot. Make six. *Off-the-Dribble; Section 8*
- **Left Side Single-Double Fade**: Start in the middle of the key. Set up a defender to the right and cut toward the left block. Imagine using a down screen (or use a cone or chair as a screener), as in a common single-double screen situation. Fade to the corner beyond the three-point line, catch and shoot. Make six. *Catch-and-Shoot; Section 15*

Right Wing America's Play and Fade Shooting Drill: Start on the right block. Turn and set a cross screen in the middle of the key. Sprint to the top of the key, catch the pass from the right wing and shoot. After the shot, fade off a high flare screen (cone) to the left side, catch the skip pass and shoot. Repeat. Make four. *First Shot: Catch-and-Shoot; Section 12. Second Shot: Catch-and-Shoot; Section 13*

Left Wing America's Play and Fade Shooting Drill: Start on the left block. Turn and set a cross screen in the middle of the key. Sprint to the top of the key, catch the pass from the left wing and shoot. After the shot, fade off a high flare screen (cone) to the right side, catch the skip pass and shoot. Repeat. Make four. *First Shot: Catch-and-Shoot; Section 12. Second Shot: Catch-and-Shoot; Section 11*

Right Side Two-Dribble Pull-up and Curl Shooting Drill: Start on the right wing outside the three-point line. Take two dribbles toward the baseline and shoot a mid-range jump shot. Finish the shot, curl to the three-point line beyond the left elbow, catch and shoot. Make six. *First Shot: Off-the-dribble; Section 5. Second Shot: Catch-and-Shoot; Section 13*

Left Side Two-Dribble Pull-up and Curl Shooting Drill: Start on the left wing outside the three-point line. Take two dribbles toward the baseline and shoot a mid-range jump shot. Finish the shot, curl to the three-point line beyond the right elbow, catch and shoot. Make six. *First Shot: Off-the-dribble; Section 7. Second Shot: Catch-and-Shoot; Section 11*

Right Side Two-Dribble Pull-up and Fade Shooting Drill: Start on the right wing outside the three-point line. Take two dribbles with the left hand toward the elbow and shoot a mid-range jump shot. Finish the shot, fade to the right wing, catch and shoot. Make six. *First Shot: Off-the-Dribble; Section 5. Second Shot: Catch-and-Shoot; Section 10*

Left Side Two-Dribble Pull-up and Fade Shooting Drill: Start on the left wing outside the three-point line. Take two dribbles with the right hand toward the elbow and shoot a mid-range jump shot. Finish the shot, fade to the left wing, catch and shoot. Make six. *First Shot: Off-the-Dribble; Section 7. Second Shot: Catch-and-Shoot; Section 14*

16 Shooting Drill: Shoot from four spots (the baseline on either side and the wing/guard position on either side). Move quickly from spot to spot. Never shoot at the baseline twice in a row. Shoot 16 shots (5 times around the arc). Set a goal. *Catch-and-Shoot; Section 9, 11, 13 and 15*

Double Move Shooting Series

- **Through-the-Legs-Crossover (right side):** Start with a right hand dribble on the right side of the court attacking toward the three-point line. Make a through-the-legs-crossover move and shoot directly off the move. Use the second move to separate from the defender. *Off-the-Dribble; Section 5*
- **Inside Hand Through-the-Legs-Crossover (right side):** Start with a left hand dribble on the right side of the court attacking toward the three-point line. Make a through-the-legs-crossover move and shoot directly off the move. Use the second move to separate from the defender. *Off-the-Dribble; Section 5*
- **Through-the-Legs-Crossover (left side):** Start with a left hand dribble on the left side of the court attacking toward the three-point line. Make a through-the-legs-crossover move and shoot directly off the move. Use the second move to separate from the defender. *Off-the-Dribble; Section 7*
- **Inside Hand Through-the-Legs-Crossover (left side):** Start with a right hand dribble on the left side of the court attacking toward the three-point line. Make a through-the-legs-crossover move and shoot directly off the move. Use the second move to separate from the defender. *Off-the-Dribble; Section 7*
- **Behind-the-Back-Crossover (right side):** Start with a right hand dribble on the right side of the court attacking toward the three-point line. Make a behind-the-back-crossover move and shoot directly off the move. Use the second move to separate from the defender. *Off-the-Dribble; Section 5*
- **Inside Hand Behind-the-Back-Crossover (right side):** Start with a left hand dribble on the right side of the court attacking toward the three-point line. Make a behind-the-back-crossover move and shoot directly off the move. Use the second move to separate from the defender. *Off-the-Dribble; Section 5*
- **Behind-the-Back-Crossover (left side):** Start with a left hand dribble on the left side of the court attacking toward the three-point line. Make a behind-the-back-crossover move and shoot directly off the move. Use the second move to separate from the defender. *Off-the-Dribble; Section 7*
- **Inside Hand Behind-the-Back-Crossover (left side):** Start with a right hand dribble on the left side of the court attacking toward the three-point line. Make a behind-the-back-crossover move and shoot directly off the move. Use the second move to separate from the defender. *Off-the-Dribble; Section 7*
- **Through-the-Legs-Behind-the-Back (right side):** Start with a right hand dribble on the right side of the court attacking toward the three-point line. Make a through-the-legs-behind-the-back move and shoot directly off the move. Use the second move to separate from the defender. *Off-the-Dribble; Section 5*
- **Inside Hand Through-the-Legs-Behind-the-Back (right side):** Start with a left hand dribble on the right side of the court attacking toward the three-point line. Make a through-

the-legs-behind-the-back move and shoot directly off the move. Use the second move to separate from the defender. *Off-the-Dribble; Section 5*

- **Through-the-Legs-Behind-the-Back (left side):** Start with a left hand dribble on the left side of the court attacking toward the three-point line. Make a through-the-legs-behind-the-back move and shoot directly off the move. Use the second move to separate from the defender. *Off-the-Dribble; Section 7*
- **Inside Hand Through-the-Legs-Behind-the-Back (left side):** Start with a right hand dribble on the left side of the court attacking toward the three-point line. Make a through-the-legs-behind-the-back move and shoot directly off the move. Use the second move to separate from the defender. *Off-the-Dribble; Section 7*

20:00 Shooting Drill: Start with the Mikan Drill. Make 20. Go to "Around the World." Make 2 shots from each block, each second hash, each elbow and then a free throw. If you miss and the rebound hits the ground, start over. Then, start at one elbow and make a lay-up and then hit the other elbow and make a lay-up. Make 20 lay-ups. Make 5 elbow jumpers in a row. Shoot three-pointers for the remainder of the time and rebound own miss. *Competitive Drill; timed.*

Phase 5

Freeze J Shooting Drill

- **Right Hand, Right Side Freeze J:** Start near half court on the right side. Attack the three-point line slowly with a right-hand dribble. Fake the drive and step in for a shot. *Off-the-dribble; Section 11*
- **Left Hand, Right Side Freeze J:** Start near half court on the right side. Attack the three-point line slowly with a left-hand dribble. Fake the drive and step in for a shot. *Off-the-dribble; Section 11*
- **Right Hand, Middle Freeze J:** Start near half court in the center of the court. Attack the three-point line slowly with a right-hand dribble. Fake the drive and step in for a shot. *Off-the-dribble; Section 12*
- **Left Hand, Middle Freeze J:** Start near half court in the center of the court. Attack the three-point line slowly with a left-hand dribble. Fake the drive and step in for a shot. *Off-the-dribble; Section 12*
- **Right Hand, Left Side Freeze J:** Start near half court on the left side. Attack the three-point line slowly with a right-hand dribble. Fake the drive and step in for a shot. *Off-the-dribble; Section 13*
- **Left Hand, Left Side Freeze J:** Start near half court on the left side. Attack the three-point line slowly with a left-hand dribble. Fake the drive and step in for a shot. *Off-the-dribble; Section 13*

One-Dribble Step-back Shooting Series

- **Middle Direct Drive One-Dribble Step-Back Drill (left pivot):** Start at the free throw line; shot fake, make a direct drive with the right foot, take one dribble with the right hand toward the basket, step-back off the left foot in the shape of a V, land and shoot. *Off-the Dribble; Section 6*
- **Middle Crossover Drive One-Dribble Step-Back Drill (left pivot):** Start at the free throw line; shot fake, make a crossover drive with the right foot, take one dribble with the left hand

toward the basket, step-back off the right foot in the shape of a V, land and shoot. *Off-the Dribble; Section 6*

- **Middle Direct Drive One-Dribble Step-Back Drill (right pivot):** Start at the free throw line; shot fake, make a direct drive with the left foot, take one dribble with the left hand toward the basket, step-back off the right foot in the shape of a V, land and shoot. *Off-the Dribble; Section 6*

- **Middle Crossover Drive One-Dribble Step-Back Drill (right pivot):** Start at the free throw line; shot fake, make a crossover drive with the left foot, take one dribble with the right hand toward the basket, step-back off the left foot in the shape of a V, land and shoot. *Off-the Dribble; Section 6*

- **Right Wing Direct Drive One-Dribble Step-Back Drill (left pivot):** Start on the right wing; shot fake, make a direct drive with the right foot, take one dribble with the right hand toward the basket, step-back off the left foot in the shape of a V, land and shoot. *Off-the Dribble; Section 5*

- **Right Wing Crossover Drive One-Dribble Step-Back Drill (left pivot):** Start on the right wing; shot fake, make a crossover drive with the right foot, take one dribble with the left hand toward the basket, step-back off the right foot in the shape of a V, land and shoot. *Off-the Dribble; Section 5*

- **Right Wing Direct Drive One-Dribble Step-Back Drill (right pivot):** Start on the right wing; shot fake, make a direct drive with the left foot, take one dribble with the left hand toward the basket, step-back off the right foot in the shape of a V, land and shoot. *Off-the Dribble; Section 5*

- **Right Wing Crossover Drive One-Dribble Step-Back Drill (right pivot):** Start on the right wing; shot fake, make a crossover drive with the left foot, take one dribble with the right hand toward the basket, step-back off the left foot in the shape of a V, land and shoot. *Off-the Dribble; Section 5*

- **Left Wing Direct Drive One-Dribble Step-Back Drill (left pivot):** Start on the left wing; shot fake, make a direct drive with the right foot, take one dribble with the right hand toward the basket, step-back off the left foot in the shape of a V, land and shoot. *Off-the Dribble; Section 7*

- **Left Wing Crossover Drive One-Dribble Step-Back Drill (left pivot):** Start on the left wing; shot fake, make a crossover drive with the right foot, take one dribble with the left hand toward the basket, step-back off the right foot in the shape of a V, land and shoot. *Off-the Dribble; Section 7*

- **Left Wing Direct Drive One-Dribble Step-Back Drill (right pivot):** Start on the left wing; shot fake, make a direct drive with the left foot, take one dribble with the left hand toward the basket, step-back off the right foot in the shape of a V, land and shoot. *Off-the Dribble; Section 7*

- **Left Wing Crossover Drive One-Dribble Step-Back Drill (right pivot):** Start on the left wing; shot fake, make a crossover drive with the left foot, take one dribble with the right hand toward the basket, step-back off the left foot in the shape of a V, land and shoot. *Off-the Dribble; Section 7*

- **Right Baseline Direct Drive One-Dribble Step-Back Drill (left pivot):** Start in the right corner; shot fake, make a direct drive with the right foot, take one dribble with the right hand toward the basket, step-back off the left foot in the shape of a V, land and shoot. *Off-the Dribble; Section 4*

- **Right Baseline Crossover Drive One-Dribble Step-Back Drill (left pivot):** Start in the right corner; shot fake, make a crossover drive with the right foot, take one dribble with the left hand toward the basket, step-back off the right foot in the shape of a V, land and shoot. *Off-the Dribble; Section 4*
- **Right Baseline Direct Drive One-Dribble Step-Back Drill (right pivot):** Start in the right corner; shot fake, make a direct drive with the left foot, take one dribble with the left hand toward the basket, step-back off the right foot in the shape of a V, land and shoot. *Off-the Dribble; Section 4*
- **Right Baseline Crossover Drive One-Dribble Step-Back Drill (right pivot):** Start in the right corner; shot fake, make a crossover drive with the left foot, take one dribble with the right hand toward the basket, step-back off the left foot in the shape of a V, land and shoot. *Off-the Dribble; Section 4*
- **Left Baseline Direct Drive One-Dribble Step-Back Drill (left pivot):** Start in the left corner; shot fake, make a direct drive with the right foot, take one dribble with the right hand toward the basket, step-back off the left foot in the shape of a V, land and shoot. *Off-the Dribble; Section 8*
- **Left Baseline Crossover Drive One-Dribble Step-Back Drill (left pivot):** Start in the left corner; shot fake, make a crossover drive with the right foot, take one dribble with the left hand toward the basket, step-back off the right foot in the shape of a V, land and shoot. *Off-the Dribble; Section 8*
- **Left Baseline Direct Drive One-Dribble Step-Back Drill (right pivot):** Start in the left corner; shot fake, make a direct drive with the left foot, take one dribble with the left hand toward the basket, step-back off the right foot in the shape of a V, land and shoot. *Off-the Dribble; Section 8*
- **Left Baseline Crossover Drive One-Dribble Step-Back Drill (right pivot):** Start in the left corner; shot fake, make a crossover drive with the left foot, take one dribble with the right hand toward the basket, step-back off the left foot in the shape of a V, land and shoot. *Off-the Dribble; Section 8*

One-Dribble Step-back 3-point Shooting Series

- **Middle Direct Drive One-Dribble 3-point Step-Back Drill (left pivot):** Start at the top of the key; shot fake, make a direct drive with the right foot, take one dribble with the right hand toward the basket, step-back off the left foot in the shape of a V, land beyond the three-point line and shoot. *Off-the Dribble; Section 12*
- **Middle Crossover Drive One-Dribble 3-point Step-Back Drill (left pivot):** Start at the top of the key; shot fake, make a crossover drive with the right foot, take one dribble with the left hand toward the basket, step-back off the right foot in the shape of a V, land beyond the three-point line and shoot. *Off-the Dribble; Section 12*
- **Middle Direct Drive One-Dribble 3-point Step-Back Drill (right pivot):** Start at the top of the key; shot fake, make a direct drive with the left foot, take one dribble with the left hand toward the basket, step-back off the right foot in the shape of a V, land beyond the three-point line and shoot. *Off-the Dribble; Section 12*
- **Middle Crossover Drive One-Dribble 3-point Step-Back Drill (right pivot):** Start at the top of the key; shot fake, make a crossover drive with the left foot, take one dribble with the right hand toward the basket, step-back off the left foot in the shape of a V, land beyond the three-point line and shoot. *Off-the Dribble; Section 12*

- **Right Wing Direct Drive One-Dribble 3-point Step-Back Drill (left pivot):** Start on the right wing beyond the three-point line; shot fake, make a direct drive with the right foot, take one dribble with the right hand toward the basket, step-back off the left foot in the shape of a V, land beyond the three-point line and shoot. *Off-the Dribble; Section 10*
- **Right Wing Crossover Drive 3-point One-Dribble Step-Back Drill (left pivot):** Start on the right wing beyond the three-point line; shot fake, make a crossover drive with the right foot, take one dribble with the left hand toward the basket, step-back off the right foot in the shape of a V, land beyond the three-point line and shoot. *Off-the Dribble; Section 10*
- **Right Wing Direct Drive One-Dribble 3-point Step-Back Drill (right pivot):** Start on the right wing beyond the three-point line; shot fake, make a direct drive with the left foot, take one dribble with the left hand toward the basket, step-back off the right foot in the shape of a V, land beyond the three-point line and shoot. *Off-the Dribble; Section 10*
- **Right Wing Crossover Drive One-Dribble 3-point Step-Back Drill (right pivot):** Start on the right wing beyond the three-point line; shot fake, make a crossover drive with the left foot, take one dribble with the right hand toward the basket, step-back off the left foot in the shape of a V, land beyond the three-point line and shoot. *Off-the Dribble; Section 10*
- **Left Wing Direct Drive One-Dribble 3-point Step-Back Drill (left pivot):** Start on the left wing beyond the three-point line; shot fake, make a direct drive with the right foot, take one dribble with the right hand toward the basket, step-back off the left foot in the shape of a V, land beyond the three-point line and shoot. *Off-the Dribble; Section 14*
- **Left Wing Crossover Drive One-Dribble 3-point Step-Back Drill (left pivot):** Start on the left wing beyond the three-point line; shot fake, make a crossover drive with the right foot, take one dribble with the left hand toward the basket, step-back off the right foot in the shape of a V, land beyond the three-point line and shoot. *Off-the Dribble; Section 14*
- **Left Wing Direct Drive One-Dribble 3-point Step-Back Drill (right pivot):** Start on the left wing beyond the three-point line; shot fake, make a direct drive with the left foot, take one dribble with the left hand toward the basket, step-back off the right foot in the shape of a V, land beyond the three-point line and shoot. *Off-the Dribble; Section 14*
- **Left Wing Crossover Drive One-Dribble 3-point Step-Back Drill (right pivot):** Start on the left wing beyond the three-point line; shot fake, make a crossover drive with the left foot, take one dribble with the right hand toward the basket, step-back off the left foot in the shape of a V, land beyond the three-point line and shoot. *Off-the Dribble; Section 14*
- **Right Baseline Direct Drive One-Dribble 3-point Step-Back Drill (left pivot):** Start in the right corner beyond the three-point line; shot fake, make a direct drive with the right foot, take one dribble with the right hand toward the basket, step-back off the left foot in the shape of a V, land beyond the three-point line and shoot. *Off-the Dribble; Section 9*
- **Right Baseline Crossover Drive One-Dribble 3-point Step-Back Drill (left pivot):** Start in the right corner beyond the three-point line; shot fake, make a crossover drive with the right foot, take one dribble with the left hand toward the basket, step-back off the right foot in the shape of a V, land beyond the three-point line and shoot. *Off-the Dribble; Section 9*
- **Right Baseline Direct Drive One-Dribble 3-point Step-Back Drill (right pivot):** Start in the right corner beyond the three-point line; shot fake, make a direct drive with the left foot, take one dribble with the left hand toward the basket, step-back off the right foot in the shape of a V, land beyond the three-point line and shoot. *Off-the Dribble; Section 9*
- **Right Baseline Crossover Drive One-Dribble 3-point Step-Back Drill (right pivot):** Start in the right corner beyond the three-point line; shot fake, make a crossover drive with

the left foot, take one dribble with the right hand toward the basket, step-back off the left foot in the shape of a V, land beyond the three-point line and shoot. *Off-the Dribble; Section 9*

- **Left Baseline Direct Drive One-Dribble 3-point Step-Back Drill (left pivot):** Start in the left corner beyond the three-point line; shot fake, make a direct drive with the right foot, take one dribble with the right hand toward the basket, step-back off the left foot in the shape of a V, land beyond the three-point line and shoot. *Off-the Dribble; Section 15*
- **Left Baseline Crossover Drive One-Dribble 3-point Step-Back Drill (left pivot):** Start in the left corner beyond the three-point line; shot fake, make a crossover drive with the right foot, take one dribble with the left hand toward the basket, step-back off the right foot in the shape of a V, land beyond the three-point line and shoot. *Off-the Dribble; Section 15*
- **Left Baseline Direct Drive One-Dribble 3-point Step-Back Drill (right pivot):** Start in the left corner beyond the three-point line; shot fake, make a direct drive with the left foot, take one dribble with the left hand toward the basket, step-back off the right foot in the shape of a V, land beyond the three-point line and shoot. *Off-the Dribble; Section 15*
- **Left Baseline Crossover Drive One-Dribble 3-point Step-Back Drill (right pivot):** Start in the left corner beyond the three-point line; shot fake, make a crossover drive with the left foot, take one dribble with the right hand toward the basket, step-back off the left foot in the shape of a V, land beyond the three-point line and shoot. *Off-the Dribble; Section 15*

Inside Pivot One-Dribble Step-Back Series

- **Inside Pivot Sweep One-Dribble Step-Backs (right side):** Start on the right block; make an L-cut to catch the pass on the right wing beyond the three-point line. Make a reverse inside pivot move with the right foot as the pivot foot. Sweep the ball and step with the left foot toward the middle of the court. Take one dribble, step-back off the right foot and shoot. *Off-the Dribble; Section 11*
- **Inside Pivot Jab-and-Crossover Drive One-Dribble Step-Backs (right side):** Start on the right block; make an L-cut to catch the pass on the right wing beyond the three-point line. Make a reverse inside pivot with the right foot as the pivot foot. Sweep the ball and jab to the middle of the court with the left foot. Make a crossover drive with the left foot and take one dribble with the right hand. Step back off the left foot and shoot. *Off-the Dribble; Section 10*
- **Inside Pivot Sweep One-Dribble Step-Backs (left side):** Start on the left block; make an L-cut to catch the pass on the left wing beyond the three-point line. Make a reverse inside pivot move with the left foot as the pivot foot. Sweep the ball and step with the right foot toward the middle of the court. Take one dribble, step-back off the left foot and shoot. *Off-the Dribble; Section 13*
- **Inside Pivot Jab-and-Crossover Drive One-Dribble Step-Backs (left side):** Start on the left block; make an L-cut to catch the pass on the left wing beyond the three-point line. Make a reverse inside pivot with the left foot as the pivot foot. Sweep the ball and jab to the middle of the court with the right foot. Make a crossover drive with the right foot and take one dribble with the left hand. Step back off the right foot and shoot. *Off-the Dribble; Section 14*

3-point Corner Curl Step-Back Series

- **3-point Corner Curl (right side):** Start in the right corner and curl to the three-point line beyond the elbow, catch and shoot. Jog to the corner and repeat. Make five. *Catch-and-Shoot*

- **3-point Corner Curl and Crossover Drive One-Dribble Step-back (right side):** Start in the right corner and curl to the three-point line beyond the elbow, catch, shot fake, use a crossover step with the left foot and one dribble with the right hand, step-back off the left foot and shoot. Make five. *Off-the Dribble; Section 11*
- **3-point Corner Curl and Run-Through One-Dribble Step-back (right side):** Start in the right corner and curl to the three-point line beyond the elbow, run through the catch, using one dribble with the left hand to separate, step back off the right foot and shoot. *Off-the Dribble; Section 12*
- **3-point Corner Curl (left side):** Start in the left corner and curl to the three-point line beyond the elbow, catch and shoot. Jog to the corner and repeat. Make five. *Catch-and-Shoot; Section 13*
- **3-point Corner Curl and Crossover Drive One-Dribble Step-back (left side):** Start in the left corner and curl to the three-point line beyond the elbow, catch, shot fake, use a crossover step with the right foot and one dribble with the left hand, step-back off the right foot and shoot. Make five. *Off-the Dribble; Section 13*
- **3-point Corner Curl and Run-Through One-Dribble Step-back (left side):** Start in the left corner and curl to the three-point line beyond the elbow, run through the catch, using one dribble with the right hand to separate, step back off the left foot and shoot. *Off-the Dribble; Section 12*

Team Drills

Phase 1

Confidence Shooting Drill: Team stands in a line at the block. Each player shoots until the team makes a certain number, say 10. Then shoot from the opposite block. Next shoot from midway up the free throw line on both sides and then the elbows. Finish with free throws. *Form Shooting; Sections 2 and 6*

Five-Star Shooting Drill: Form five lines: one under the basket (with ball), two off the elbows and two off the baseline. Player 1 under the basket throws to P2 at the elbow and follows his/her pass. P2 passes to the player at the opposite baseline (Player 3), who passes to the other baseline player (Player 4). P4 passes to Player 5 at the opposite elbow and P5 shoots. The next player in line under the basket rebounds the ball and passes to P1. *Catch and Shoot; Section 6*

Seven Free Throw Shooting Drill: Players form line along free throw line. Each player starts with seven points. Players can only lose points: once a point is lost, they cannot gain the point back. First shot is worth nothing: if player misses, he goes to the end of the line without consequence. If he makes the shot, the next shot is worth 1. If Player 2, shooting next, misses the shot, he loses a point and goes to the end of the line and Player 3 shoots with nothing on the line. If P2 makes the shot, then P3's shot is worth two points. Last player with points left is winner. *Form Shooting/Free Throws*

Oiler Shooting Drill: Four players form a line at the top of the key; the first player does not have a ball, but the other three do. Player 1 sprints to the baseline, stops, pivots and runs toward the line, receiving the pass in the lane. He pivots, shoots and rebounds his shot. Player 2 passes to P1 and sprints to the baseline, completing the same drill as P1. Use same pattern to shoot a variety of shots. *Catch-and-Shoot; Section 6*

Oiler Kick-out Shooting Drill: Form a line at the top of the key with one player starting on the wing. Player 1 passes to wing (P2) and cuts to the ball side post. P2 passes to P1 and relocates. P1 passes to P2 for the jump shot. P1 cuts to be the next wing and receives the pass from P3, while P2 retrieves the rebound and runs to the end of the line. *Catch-and-Shoot; Sections 4 and 8*

Phase 2

Sooner Fast Break Shooting Drill: Five players make a line at the free throw line, facing towards half court. Player 2 and 3 have balls. Player 1 runs to half court, cuts to the sideline at a 45-degree angle, touches the sideline and cuts toward the basket at a 45-degree angle. P2 passes to P1 who shoots. P2 sprints to half court. P1 rebounds and hands to P4. Shoot within your range. *Catch-and-Shoot; Sections 5 and 7*

Team Corner Curls Shooting Drill: Form one line at the left elbow and one line in the right corner. First shooter curls from the right corner to the right elbow and receives the pass. He rebounds. Passer and shooter switch lines. *Catch-and-Shoot; Section 6*

Surf Shooting Drill: Start with 2 lines, one at each intersection of the lane line and the baseline. Use three balls. Use coach, chair or cone as marker to run around. P1 curls around the cone, receives pass from P2 and shoots. After making pass, P2 runs behind P1, curls and receives pass from P3. Players rebound own shot, change lines and return ball to the front of the line to which they are going. Move the cone back every 20 shots. *Catch-and-Shoot; Sections 2 and 6*

Spot-to-Spot Shooting Drill: Player 1 shoots, Player 2 passes and Player 3 rebounds. Use two balls. P1 shoots and cuts from the elbow to the baseline. P2 passes P1 the second ball, while P3 rebounds the first ball and passes to P2. P1 shoots and cuts to the elbow. Shoot from different areas on the floor and from different passing angles. Make ten and rotate. *Catch-and-Shoot; Sections 4, 6 and 8*

8:00 Shooting Drill: In three or four-man groups, groups must make 35 shots from each block; 35 shots from each elbow; and then 5 three-point shots from each of five shots. Player shoots and rebounds own shot. Drill lasts 8:00. *Form Shooting (block) and Catch-and-Shoot; Sections 1, 3, 6, 9, 10, 12, 14 and 15*

Phase 3

One-Dribble Pull-ups Team Shooting Drill: Player 1 shoots, Player 2 passes and Player 3 is a token (three-quarter speed) defender. P2 makes the skip pass to P1, and P3 closes-out to defend the initial move (defender stops on the dribble). P1 makes a shot fake (ball to eyes) and extends away from the defender with one dribble for a jump shot. Initially, have the defense closeout to force a certain direction; a couple shots to the baseline and a couple to the middle. Eventually, allow the defender to closeout without instruction so the offensive player must read the defense when making his move. Passer becomes the next defender, defender becomes the next shooter and shooter follows his shot, rebounds and takes the ball to the passing line. *Off-the-Dribble; Sections 5, 6 and 7*

Team Full Court Pull-ups: One player starts at half court and his teammates start under either basket. First player attacks the free throw line for a pull-up jumper. His teammate rebounds and attacks the other end for a pull-up jumper. The third teammate rebounds and attacks. First team to make 10 shots wins. *Off-the-Dribble; Section 6*

Phase 4

Partner Shooting Drill: Player 1 passes ball to Player 2 and closes out to the shooter. P2 shoots the ball and follows his shot to rebound. P1 contests the shot and relocates for his shot, moving continuously and calling for the ball. P2 pass to P1 and contests shot. *Catch-and-Shoot; all sections*

Utes' Shooting Drill: Set-up a chair (screener) where the player would typically receive a screen within his/her team offense and have the player work on using the screen. Player must call out his cut as he uses the screen: Flare, Loose Curl, Tight Curl or Backdoor. This teaches the player to communicate with teammates as well as getting repetitions on game-like shots. A loose curl takes the player towards the ball, while a tight curl leads the player towards the basket. A backdoor cut leads to a lay-up. *Catch-and-Shoot; all sections*

String Shooting Drill (flare): Passing line (with balls) starts on the wing, free throw line extended beyond the three-point line and shooting line starts at the top of the key. Passers penetrate middle, jump stop and pass to the shooter. The shooter flares away from the dribbler. Shooter follows his own shot and fills the line with the ball; passer fills the shooter line. *Catch-and-Shoot; Sections 5, 7, 10 and 14*

String Shooting Drill (follow): First person in passing line dribbles to the baseline, away from the Shooter, jump stops, pivots and passes to the shooter. The shooter follows (maintain spacing) and shoots. Again, shooter follows his shot and the players switch lines. The shooter must keep enough distance between he and the dribbler. Passers should work on a reverse pivot, protecting the ball from the defense. *Catch-and-Shoot; Sections 5, 7, 9, 10, 14 and 15*

Husky 35 Shooting Drill: Form three lines at half-court with two balls in the middle line. The first person in the middle line passes to the first person in one of the wing lines, and he passes across to the other wing, similar to a three-man weave. The second wing receives the pass and shoots; the team is awarded three points for a made three-pointer and two points for a made two-pointer. If the shot is a miss, and one of the three players gets the rebound in the air, they score the put back and the team is awarded one point. If the ball hits the ground, the team starts again at zero. The second group starts after the first group shoots. Goal is to get thirty-five points in two-minutes (change the time for appropriate levels). *Catch-and-Shoot; Sections 1, 3, 5, 7, 10 and 14*

Santa Cruz Shooting Drill: Form three-man teams with one teammate starting on each baseline with a ball and one at half court. Player 1 at half court sprints toward the three-point line, receives the pass, shoots and retrieves the ball, while Player 2 passes to P1 and then sprints to the other end. First team to 18 wins. *Catch-and-Shoot; Sections 10, 11, 12, 13 and 14*

Phase 5

1v1 Shooting Drill: Start a step inside the top of the key. Offensive player must stay within the half circle above the free throw line, create space and score. Defense defends without fouling. Make it, take it: play to three.

1v1 No Dribble: Start at the free throw line. Defense checks the ball to the offensive player. Offensive player must shoot without using a dribble. Make it, take it: play to three.

1v1 One Dribble: Start on the block. Offensive player makes an L-cut to the wing to receive the pass. Offensive player has one dribble to create a shot. Make it, take it: play to five.

1v1 Half Court: Start at half court. Offensive player cannot go inside the key. Use the dribble to create a shot. Make it, take it: play to five.

1v1 Three-point line: The offensive player starts at half court and the defensive player starts at the top of the key. Defense cannot leave the interior of the three-point arc. Offensive player attacks the defender, but must stay outside the key. Offense cannot shoot a three-pointer. Make it, take it: play to five.

Utes' Shooting Live: An offensive player starts at the guard spot (Player 1) and another on the wing (Player 2), each with a defender. Coach starts on the opposite guard spot. Player 1 initiates the offense with a pass to the coach. P1 either basket cuts or sets the screen for P2 near the mid-post. Once the offense receives the pass, they have one pass to create a shot. Make it, take it: play to five baskets.

T-Shirts

180Shooter.com features a series of t-shirts which represent one of the five phases in the shooting progression. Pictured above is the general t-shirt, a white t-shirt with the logo on the front and "Be a Shot Maker, not just a shot taker" on the back. The other t-shirts available at 180shooter.com:

Phase 1: Grey, "Practice in Proportion to your Aspirations."

Phase2: Green, "Practice makes Permanent."

Phase 3: Navy Blue, "Whether you think you cam or you think you can't, you're right."

Phase 4: Red, "There are two pains in life: the pain of discipline and the pain of regret: Choose."

Phase 5: Black, "Certified Shot Maker."

References

- Baum, Ken. (1999). The Mental Edge. New York: The Berkeley Publishing Group.
- Bloom, Benjamin. (1985). Developing Talent in Young People. New York: Ballantine Books.
- Branch, John. "For Free Throws, 50 Years of Practice is No Help." *New York Times*, March 3, 2009.
- Csikszentmihalyi, Mihaly, Kevin Rathunde and Samuel Whalen. (1993). Talented Teenagers: The Roots of Success & Failure. New York: Cambridge University Press.
- Dorrance, Anson. (2002). The Vision of a Champion. Ann Arbor, MI: Huron River Press.
- Drury, Bob. "Bravery (and how to master it)" *Men's Health*, April 2008.
- Dweck, Carol. (2006). Mindset. New York: Random House.
- Ericsson, K. Anders. (1996). The Road to Excellence. Mahwah New Jersey: Lawrence Erlbaum Associates, Publishers.
- Ferriss, Tim. "The Power of Less: Changing Behavior with Leo Babauta." *Four Hour Work Week* blog, January 7, 2009.
- Friedman, David. "Cleveland Romps: Cavs Smash Sonics 95-79." *20-Second Timeout*, January 9, 2008.
- Hay, J.G. (1973). The Biomechanics of Sports Techniques. Englewood Cliffs, NJ: Prentice Hall. (pp. 228-234).
- Gallwey, Timothy. (1974). The Inner Game of Tennis. New York: Random House.
- Gambetta, Vern. (2007). Athletic Development. Champaign, IL: Human Kinetics.
- Kopp, Sheldon B. (1972). If You Meet the Buddha on the Road, Kill Him! New York: Bantam Books.
- McCormick, Brian. (2007). Cross Over: The New Model of Youth Basketball Development, Second Edition. Sacramento: Brian McCormick and Lulu Press.
- McCormick, Brian. (2005). Pure: The Biomechanics and Mental Approach to Successful Shooting. North Carolina: Basketball Sense Publication.
- McDougall, Christopher. "The Science of Swish." *Men's Health*, September 2008.
- Mikes, Jay. (1987). Basketball FundaMENTALs. Champaign, IL: Human Kinetics.
- Nater, Swen and Ronald Gallimore. (2006). You Haven't Taught Until They Have Learned. Morgantown, WV: Fitness Information Technology.
- Parent, Joe. Zen Golf.
- Schmidt, Dr. Richard and Bjork, Dr. Robert A. "New Conceptualizations of Practice: Common Principles in Three Paradigms Suggest New Training Concepts." *Psychological Science*, Vol. 3, No. 4 July 1992.
- Spoelstra, Jon. (2001). Marketing Outrageously. Austin, TX: Bard Press.

About the Author

Brian McCormick is the Performance Director for TrainforHoops.com, a comprehensive, individualized, progressive online basketball training site. He played for Nassjo Basket in Sweden and coached professionally in Ireland and Sweden, where he coached in the Damligan All-Star Game and led his team to the play-offs. He has directed camps or clinics in Canada, China, Greece, Macedonia, Morocco, South Africa and Trinidad & Tobago, and coached at the college, high school, CYO and AAU levels.

McCormick received his B.A. in American Literature and Culture from UCLA, where he directed the UCLA Special Olympics program and rowed for the UCLA Crew team, and a Master's in Sports Science from the United States Sports Academy.

McCormick's articles have appeared in magazines in England, South Africa, Canada, Italy, France, Belgium and the United States. He has published seven other books: (Cross Over: The New Model of Youth Basketball Development; Blitz Basketball; Brian McCormick's Hard2Guard Player Development Newsletters, Vol. 1; Brian McCormick's Hard2Guard Player Development Newsletters, Vol. 2; Hard2Guard: Skill Development for Perimeter Players; Developing Basketball Intelligence and Championship Basketball Plays) and produced a DVD (*Great Ball Handling Made Easy*) which is available through Full Court Basketball. He writes a free weekly newsletter, *Hard2Guard Player Development Newsletters*, which is available by emailing hard2guardinc@yahoo.com.

He lives in Irvine, CA where he trains players and works as a consultant to youth basketball coaches, teams, organizations and facilities in the United States and abroad.

Made in the USA
Lexington, KY
19 May 2010